BRAND SOMETHING BEAUTIFUL

A Branding Workbook for Artists, Writers, and Other Creatives

BY STEVE BROCK

SUBLIMITY PRESS

Copyright © 2025 by Steve Brock

All rights reserved. This book or parts thereof may not be reproduced in any form, stored in any retrieval system, or transmitted in any form by any means—electronic, mechanical, photocopy, recording, or otherwise—without prior written permission of the publisher, except as provided by United States of America copyright law. For permission requests, write to the publisher, at "Attention: Permissions Coordinator," at the following address:

Sublimity Press
300 Lenora Street # 844
Seattle, WA 98121

ISBN: 978-1-7351188-8-8

Copy by Steve Brock

Cover and book design by Sumner Brock Design

All logos, trademarks, and corporate and other examples are the property of their respective owners and are used here for illustrative and educational purposes only. No affiliation or endorsement is implied.

Printed in the United States of America

First printing edition 2025

To find out about group, corporate and private-label sales of this book contact info@sublimitypress.com

1. Personal Branding 2. Art & Business 3. Entrepreneurship 4. Creativity

PRAISE FOR STEVE BROCK & *BRAND SOMETHING BEAUTIFUL*

Branding can seem like a key to a magical doorway that, once found, will unlock potential and momentum. Choosing the just-right words and images to convey the work you're doing in the world feels both crucial and overwhelming. With *Brand Something Beautiful*, Steve Brock offered me clarity and encouragement, turning all of my second-guessing into a joyful journey of discovery. With his artist's eye, patient guidance, and laughter, he invites those of us doing work of our hearts to find the language and imagery we need to both deepen our understanding of what we're truly doing—that deep why—and to widen our reach and impact in ways that do feel, yes… a little bit magic.

Naomi Kinsman
Illumineer & Founder of Creative Lift

I've had the chance to watch Steve Brock work with all kinds of clients, and honestly—he's one of the best brand strategists I've ever seen. He listens deeply, makes connections no one else would think of, and somehow turns branding into something not just practical, but powerful, simple, and even fun. Now he's captured that same magic in this book—a true gift for anyone wanting to build their brand. I immediately thought: every writer, artist, photographer, and entrepreneur I know needs a copy.

Barbara Takata
Executive Vice President, Client Engagement, Masterworks

Two great obstacles of entrepreneurship are understanding what you do and getting others to understand what you do. These both require someone or some process to help you move from that tornado-brain, tongue-tied hell to a place of clarity. Steve Brock is that someone and, in *Brand Something Beautiful,* he offers us one of the most empowering gifts a creator can receive---the ability to clearly see yourself and your work.

Marlita Hill
Choreographer and author of *Nail that Niche*

More than a branding workbook, *Brand Something Beautiful* is a guide for creatives who know they have something meaningful to share but need to assemble a clear plan for how to connect it to the world. Steve Brock has taken decades of experience and distilled it into a practical, inspiring, and deeply accessible process that guides artists, writers, and makers to move from vision to voice to value.

I've worked at the epicenter of culture, arts, and social movements for over twenty years, and I can say with confidence that this is one of the most useful, actionable, and encouraging resources I've seen for creatives. If you want to stop guessing about your brand and start building something that truly resonates, this book belongs on your desk.

Erik Løkkesmoe
Creative Strategist for entertainment, government, and social impact

Back when I was just a baby thinking about turning 30, Steve Brock took me under his wing and gave me a world-class education in branding. It changed my life and has shaped every business I've built and every ounce of communication with my audience. *Brand Something Beautiful* is your chance to be mentored by one of the most brilliant minds in branding and marketing. Steve Brock provides not only clear, decisive information about why branding matters, but also the key exercises and thought experiments you need to create your unique brand and bring your creative work to your audience. Start at the beginning, do it all—and it will change your creative life and business.

Michelle Mays
Author of *The Betrayal Bind*

Some of the many brands Steve Brock has worked with:

CONTENTS

PART 1: DETERMINE 1
PART 2: DISCOVER 15
PART 3: DEFINE 35
PART 4: DESIGN 65
PART 5: DELIGHT 103
APPENDIX: BRAND ARCHITECTURE 118
REFERENCES 123
NEED ADDITIONAL HELP? 124
ABOUT THE AUTHOR 125

THE ROAD AHEAD: WHAT WE'LL COVER

 1. DETERMINE *WHERE YOU'RE GOING*

What is a brand? ▶ What is branding? ▶ Why your creative brand matters

---

 2. DISCOVER

YOU: Who you are and what you want
- What do you desire to do creatively?
- What distinguishes you (how are you different)?
- What do you believe (values) and why do you exist (purpose)?

THEM: Who they are and what they want
- Understanding your favorite fan
- Understanding their drives and desires
- Listening to them

3. DEFINE *YOUR BRAND IDENTITY*

Your Big Idea ▶ Your Secret Sauce ▶ Your Personality and Voice ▶

▶ Your offerings and how you make people feel ▶ Your Role ▶ Your Positioning ▶ Your Special Resource

---

 ## 4. DESIGN *YOUR VERBAL & VISUAL IDENTITIES*

What you say & how you say it ▶ Your look & feel ▶ Your brand book & artifacts

---

 ## 5. DELIGHT *APPLYING THE BRAND*

Website ▶ Social Media ▶ Email ▶ Events ▶ Meetings & Presentations ▶

▶ Products & Services ▶ Signage ▶ Marketing Ads & Materials ▶ Videos ▶ Content

KNOW BEFORE YOU GO

Throughout the book you'll see these icons in the sidebars. They provide additional insights, context, and ideas. In particular, look for the Essential icon. It signifies a key part of your brand.

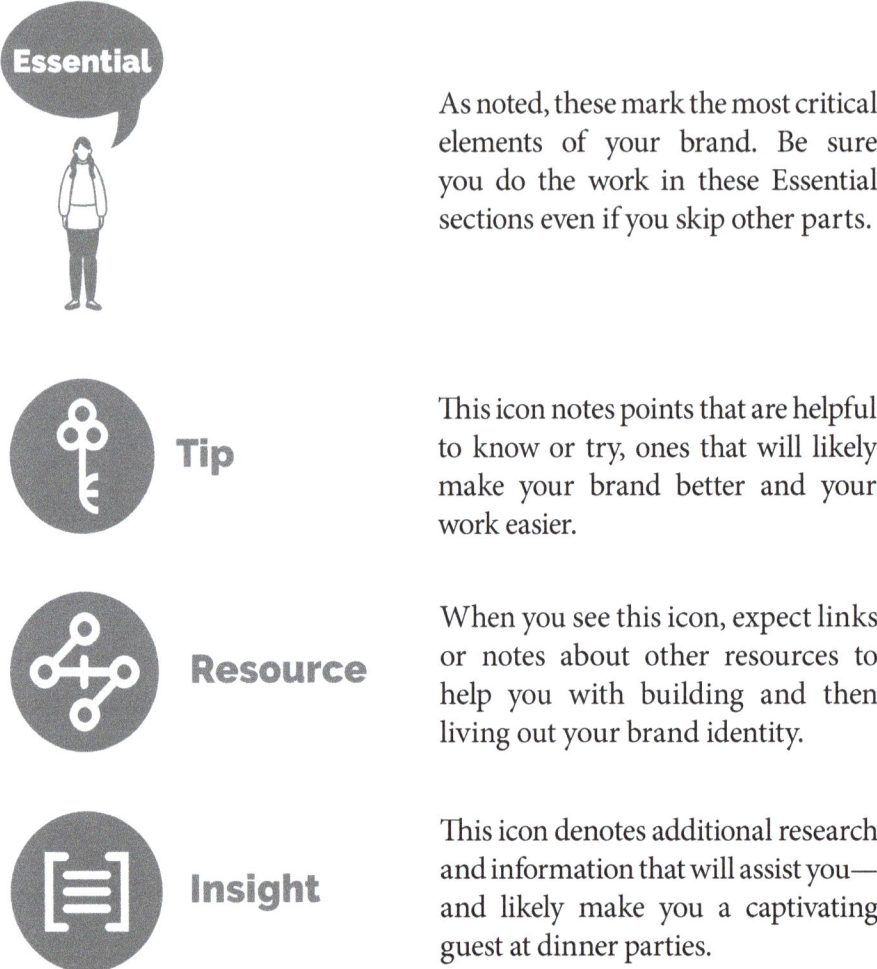

As noted, these mark the most critical elements of your brand. Be sure you do the work in these Essential sections even if you skip other parts.

This icon notes points that are helpful to know or try, ones that will likely make your brand better and your work easier.

When you see this icon, expect links or notes about other resources to help you with building and then living out your brand identity.

This icon denotes additional research and information that will assist you—and likely make you a captivating guest at dinner parties.

Most of all, be sure to go to www.BrandSomethingBeautiful.com to get your free digital worksheets (so you don't have to write everything by hand in this book unless you prefer that approach), as well as other resources and links to the sites noted throughout this book.

PART 1:
DETERMINE

DETERMINE *WHERE YOU'RE GOING*

What is a brand? ▶ **What is branding?** ▶ **Why your creative brand matters**

LET'S GET STARTED

The first step in developing a brand for your creative work is to determine if you should. Maybe you already know you need a brand. Or maybe you suspect you might. Or others have told you how important it is. Or you're tired of influencers on Instagram and TikTok talking about working their brands and you have no idea what they mean (assuming they do). Or maybe you're not sure about any of this. No worries. We'll start here by covering all the reasons building a brand can help and why it is worth the effort.

The simplest reason is this: **Branding is the missing middle between making something beautiful and marketing that work.**

Your brand goes far beyond just your marketing, but if you're like most creative (or at least artistic) people, it's the marketing aspect you probably dread most. Often that's because you haven't done the branding that will make the marketing easier. The point of this book is to help you create a brand for you and your creative work that will make the marketing and selling of your products or services not just easier, but more enjoyable. Pretty good reason, huh?

THE BIG QUESTIONS

In the following pages, we'll tackle these questions and more:

- What is a brand, what is branding, and why are they so important?
- How is branding different for artists, writers, creatives, and solopreneurs?
- How do I make the biggest impact with the least amount of work?
- How do I know what to focus on or do?
- How do I make my work distinctive and stand out amid all the noise?
- How do I help people to find out about my work?
- How do I help people to care about my work?
- How do I sell more of my work and make more money without compromising my integrity as a creator?

Insight

HOW I CAN HELP YOU

Since I'll be your guide through this book, here's a bit about me.

- I've worked with clients from Fortune 500 corporations (Microsoft, Walmart, Prudential, and others) to global nonprofits to startups to writers, artists and solopreneurs. So I know what works in a variety of contexts and how to craft brands that succeed.

- But I'm also a creator like you. On the side, I also write, photograph, paint, design furniture, compose music, and pursue many other creative interests.

- I know the difficulties and frustrations of marketing my own stuff. It's one thing for me to help a client market their work and another for me to do it myself.

- I've seen how branding can transform, and I also know why making it simple is the only way to make it stick, especially when you're not a large company.

WHAT IS A BRAND?

Let's start with the first question, what is a brand. Simply put, *your brand is the overall association or perception that a person has of you and your work.* It is much more than your logo, tagline, colors, or other messages or visuals; all those are the elements most people think of when they hear the word "brand."

For example, when you hear the names American Airlines, Ferrari, or Qdoba, you have far more associations about these brands than merely their visuals or messaging. That's because *everything you do related to your creative work and how you present that to the world affects your brand.* You can think of your brand as being like your reputation—the general opinion, esteem, or judgment people hold about a person or thing. Or like goodwill, that ineffable quality or trust you extend to someone or something.

Your brand relates both to who you are and to what you do. Put another way, *your purpose is what you do, but your brand is the distinctive way you carry out that purpose.* Many other creatives may have a similar purpose to you—to inform, enlighten, express themselves, build a business, create beauty, address a societal issue, etc.—but how you live that out in your unique way, that is your brand.

No matter what kind of brand you have (we'll cover types of brands shortly), all great brands, even for solopreneurs and small creative firms, share these attributes. Great brands are:

- **True:** Aspire to be the very best version of you and your work, but that has to be grounded in reality. You can't claim your new nonfiction book is the finest work ever written on the subject if it is derivative. What you promise, explicit or implied, must be true.

- **Distinctive**: You want to stand out from the crowd. But being different alone is not enough. You could try to shock people or do something outrageous and you'd be different. But you must also be …

- **Relevant:** You must matter to your audience. You want them to identify with you and see you and your work as being for them. The good news is that if you are highly relevant, you'll automatically be distinctive.

Everything you do as a creative will affect your brand because your brand encompasses everything you do as a creative.

- **Actionable:** Having people think good thoughts about you isn't enough for a brand. You want them to buy your products or services. Great brands compel people to act.
- **Consistent:** Even though your art or other creative work itself should evolve over time, you want the basic, positive associations people have with you to stay consistent. Otherwise, you'll never build traction.

Great brands also provide several benefits. A clear, compelling, and consistent brand:

- *Acts as a filter for making decisions.* You will know what to say yes to and, even more important, what to say no to.
- *Allows you to charge more.* Powerful brands allow companies to increase their prices. How many times have you paid more for a branded product that is essentially the same as the generic version?
- *Helps others tell your story.* When your customers or clients have a simple and clear way to describe you and your work, it's easier for them to tell others.
- *Helps you center and focus as a creator.* You likely bought this book thinking it will help you with marketing and sales. And it will. But a hidden benefit is how much a strong brand will help you know where to focus your efforts and resources and how freeing that can be.

WHAT IS BRANDING?

Now let's turn to the word branding. It's quite simple: **branding is the process of intentionally building your brand**. This includes: knowing who you are, what you offer, how you're different, why it matters to your audiences, and how to communicate it in a way that resonates and excites. A few more clarifying points:

- On a deeper level, **branding is about making it easier for people to love your work as much as you do.** That happens because branding helps people to grasp the relevance of you and your work to them.
- *Your brand only exists in the minds of your audience.* You can't force someone to love you or

> **Having a clear and compelling brand not only makes it easier for your audiences to tell others, it makes them *want* to tell others.**

CONSISTENCY AND CHANGE

It's a paradox: How do you stay consistent and evolve as a creative? By keeping the underlying core of your brand the same over time. Look at Picasso. He went through distinct stylistic periods—Blue Period, Rose Period, Cubism, Neoclassicism, Surrealism. And yet, his creative brand remained consistent. You can see throughout his works a commitment to mastery, a creative boldness, a disregard for what others thought, and ongoing curiosity about perspective and perception. His work—even his style—changed. His creative brand did not.

your work in branding any more than in dating. Thus, your job is to plant a positive memory, if you will, a sense of what you want people to think about you and your work, then, keep it alive, correct it when it goes off track, and remind people of why it matters. That may sound complicated, but it quickly becomes intuitive.

- You can't control how your audiences think or feel, but ***you can control the signals you send that contribute to how they think and feel.*** That's what branding is and does.

- Brands aren't bulletproof. They can get tarnished or fade. That's why ***you must steward your brand carefully. Build it, then protect it. Defend it. Nurture it***. And make sure it remains strong and relevant for your audiences over time. The whole final section of this book focuses on this.

Ultimately, ***branding is the art of making emotional connections to and through you and your work.*** "How can I sell more?" will always lead to an almost adversarial mindset. "How can I delight them more?" changes how you present your work and respect your audience.

Branding is your secret weapon, one that most creatives miss because they don't even know it exists or understand why they need a brand. ***Developing your brand is not about changing what you do but helping you do what you do more effectively.*** So what does developing your brand look like? Here are four general steps/phases (or five if you count the one you're currently in, DETERMINE), each of which represents a section in this book:

- **DISCOVER**: *Understand who you are (as a brand) and what you offer, as well as who your audiences are and what they want.*

- **DEFINE**: *Develop your brand identity* (much like your own identity as a person, but including the creative work you make). This is the most important step and the one most often skipped. Most people and organizations jump from learning a bit about themselves and their markets (DISCOVER) directly into making a logo and tagline, elements found in the step of DESIGN. And they pay for that later when things aren't working. Don't be that person (or organization).

- **DESIGN**: *Craft your brand's verbal identity (your voice, key messages, and story) and then its visual elements*—logo, colors, typography, symbols, photography and illustration, etc. Those lead to the artifacts you'll use (website, social media, signage, brochures, t-shirts, etc.) to represent your brand.

- **DELIGHT**: *Launch your brand and grow it.* Once you have all the pieces in place, you focus on creating *experiences of delight* so that every touchpoint with your audience becomes a meaningful and memorable encounter.

TYPES OF BRANDS

Now that you have some sense of what we mean by brand and branding, let's turn to different types of brands. They include:

- ***Organizational*** (e.g., Apple, Starbucks, Panera)
- ***Product*** (e.g., iPhone, Frappuccino, Fuji Apple Salad)
- ***Service*** (e.g., Kaiser Permanente, Gold's Gym, Jiffy Lube)
- ***Personal*** (e.g., Kim Kardashian, Josh Richards, Alix Earle)
- ***Creative*** (e.g., you AND your products)

If you're a company, you have an organizational brand that produces products and/or services. Many of these products have their own brands, but not always: generics, commodities, industrial products, and most services just use descriptions, not actual brands. Same with many artists. For example, most paintings may have titles (or even "Untitled"), but they aren't brands. These "products" don't need to be branded because, to an audience, the brand that matters most is the artist. And if that's the case, does that mean the artist needs a personal brand? The answer isn't as clear as you may think.

 Insight

WHY BRANDS FAIL

In working on brands for over 25 years, I've found *most brands fail for two reasons*:

1. *They skip DISCOVER and most of all, DEFINE, and go straight to DESIGN.* They may have a nice logo, pretty colors and beautiful imagery, but they don't know what they truly stand for or how they're distinctive.

2. *They aren't consistent in the DELIGHT phase.* They launch their brand but don't steward it well. They end up looking and sounding like everyone else.

Work through all the steps. Own your brand. Take both care of, and joy in, the building and long-term management of your brand. After all, it's the public reflection of who you are as a creator.

To understand the type of brand you need, let's start by understanding three different but related concepts: *creative identity, creative brand, and personal brand.*

YOUR CREATIVE IDENTITY

As a creative person, **you have a creative identity, something no corporation or organizational brand can match.** It's the soul of who you are creatively, a combination of your creative values, aesthetics, beliefs, style, voice, interests, and motivation. It's the source of all your creative work and the lens through which you view the world. It reflects the sources/influences, themes, questions, and perspectives that repeatedly show up in your work. You don't force or manufacture your creative identity the way you do a brand. It's just a reflection of who you are as a creative person.

We're going to spend the first part of the next chapter, DISCOVER, helping you to articulate this creative identity so you know which aspects of it to amplify with your public-facing brand. Note that hyphenated phrase, "public-facing." *If you never offer your work to be sold or even displayed to others, you still have a creative identity.* But when you shift to the marketplace, that's when you need a brand. But what type?

THE PERSONAL BRAND

A personal brand is about you, the person. In this sense, *you* are the product. A personal brand includes;

- How you show up publicly and present your work
- What story you tell others about yourself
- Where you appear (what channels and media you use)
- The ways you engage your audiences and peers and what you want from them
- Your personal style and voice

A personal brand builds on your creative identity rather than invents some new, inauthentic version of you. But the key here with a personal brand is the emphasis on you. With Oprah or MrBeast (Jimmy Donaldson), you likely know more about them as people than you do about any specific creative work they've made.

REMEMBER WHY YOU DO THIS

As you develop your creative brand, it's easy to get caught up in the brand and publicly-facing aspects of what you do. So even if you feel you understand your creative identity well, I encourage you to take time working through the exercises in the DISCOVER: YOU section of the next chapter. Not just for your brand, but to help you reconnect to all the things you love about creating. We all need that reminder periodically.

THE CREATIVE BRAND

With a creative brand, the focus is on your work. It still has to reflect you and your creative identity, but the emphasis is more about the output of your creativity rather than the person behind it. Think about popular creatives such as Malcolm Gladwell or Donna Tartt (who rarely gives interviews or reveals anything about her private life), or especially Banksy (since we know nothing about the person behind the street art). You know them more by their products than by their latest choice in restaurants or moisturizer.

In some cases, because creative brands are about you AND the creative products you make, it's hard for your audiences to separate the two. Some fans will know a great deal about the personal life of Billie Eilish or Stephen King. Others, however, might know every word to "Everything I Wanted" or the order of short stories in King's *Night Shift* but wouldn't recognize either artist on the street.

One of the benefits of creative brands is that they allow you to separate you as a person from you as a brand. You get to keep your private life private if you want. Moreover, if one of your pieces doesn't take off, it isn't as personal because the work is just something you make. It isn't you.

The best news is that you can decide how much of a personal brand (meaning how much you want to show up personally in the public's eye) you want to develop. *The overlap between personal brand and creative brand is entirely up to you.* And it's not a decision you have to make immediately. Maybe you start with a focus entirely on your products and services but over time, you find you enjoy public speaking and have become a thought leader in your field. In that case, you just lean into the personal brand more while not abandoning your creative identity.

To give you a better sense of how all this fits together, take a look at the following table. It summarizes the differences between a creative identity, a creative brand, and a personal brand. Use it to help you understand the differences so you can determine which approach is best for you.

IT'S UP TO YOU

How much you want to promote yourself (i.e. build a personal brand), as well as your work, is your choice. It's a decision most creatives grow into over time, so don't worry too much now about whether your focus is more on a creative brand or a personal one. Just build the brand using this workbook in the way that feels most authentic to you.

	CREATIVE IDENTITY	CREATIVE BRAND	PERSONAL BRAND
Focus:	Internal (self-driven)	External (audience and product-focused)	External (audience and person-focused but may include products)
Purpose:	Self-expression & exploration	Public recognition, engagement, connection	Public influence, trust, career advancement
Characteristics:	Personal creative vision, style, voice, medium	Public identity, look, feel, & messaging for marketing creative work	Public identity, look, feel, & messaging for marketing presence as a person
Examples:	Frida Kahlo's early symbolic work	Lisa Congdon's colorful illustrations	Austin Kleon's role as artist, author, curator, and speaker

If any of this differentiation between a personal brand and a creative one still seems murky, don't worry. What you call it doesn't matter. What you do with it does. *As a creative, you're representing you and the work you make.* And its that combination that we'll focus on in this book.

MOVING FORWARD

My intent here isn't to make you an expert on branding. It's to provide a workbook and proven process to help you craft your creative brand. You'll learn a great deal about branding along the way, but the primary objective for you as a maker is to make this thing known as YOUR brand. Your creative brand.

You'll get the knowhow here in the following pages. And if you want it even easier, try the following ***Quick Start Guide for Impatient Creatives***. Glance through the choices and see if there are any sections you already feel you know well. It's for those wanting the fastest way through this branding process.

My advice, however, is to just plow through this book from start to finish. Not because I want to make it harder. Just the opposite. While this approach may take a bit more time now, it will save you so much time, effort, and resources later because you'll have considered all the elements that affect your creative brand, and ultimately the underlying issues that will affect the marketing of your creative work. As you go, you may find sections that feel similar to others you've already done. That's intentional. Not to be repetitive, but so you learn how to frame your brand from a variety of perspectives.

And for you Goldilocks fans who want a happy medium between reading every word and skipping vast swaths of remarkable content, don't forget that I've marked certain sections as "**Essential.**" At the very least, skim through the whole book but stop when you see the Essential icon and work on those.

Are you ready and determined to move on? Then let's start by discovering the critical aspects of your creative identity so you'll know which ones to emphasize as you build your creative brand.

EVERYTHING YOU NEED

In case you were so excited to dive in and you missed the QR code earlier, here it is for BrandSomethingBeautiful.com. It's your go-to place for a digital version of all the worksheets used for this book and a wealth of other resources and links. You'll even find bonus content like articles and guides that I couldn't fit into this book.

QUICK START GUIDE
REGARDING YOUR CREATIVE WORK OR BUSINESS...

I know who I am creatively and what I want to do	NO ▶	Go to Desire, p. 18

YES ▼

I know what makes me distinctive in the marketplace	NO ▶	Go to Distinction, p. 21

YES ▼

I know what I believe and why I exist	NO ▶	Go to Values & Purpose, p. 27

YES ▼

I know who my audiences are and what they want	NO ▶	Go to DISCOVER: THEM, p. 30

YES ▼

I know my brand's essence	NO ▶	Go to Brand Essence, p. 40

YES ▼

I know my brand's promise	NO ▶	Go to Brand Promise, p. 45

YES ▼

I know my brand's features and benefits	NO ▶	Go to Offering, Features, & Benefits, p. 48

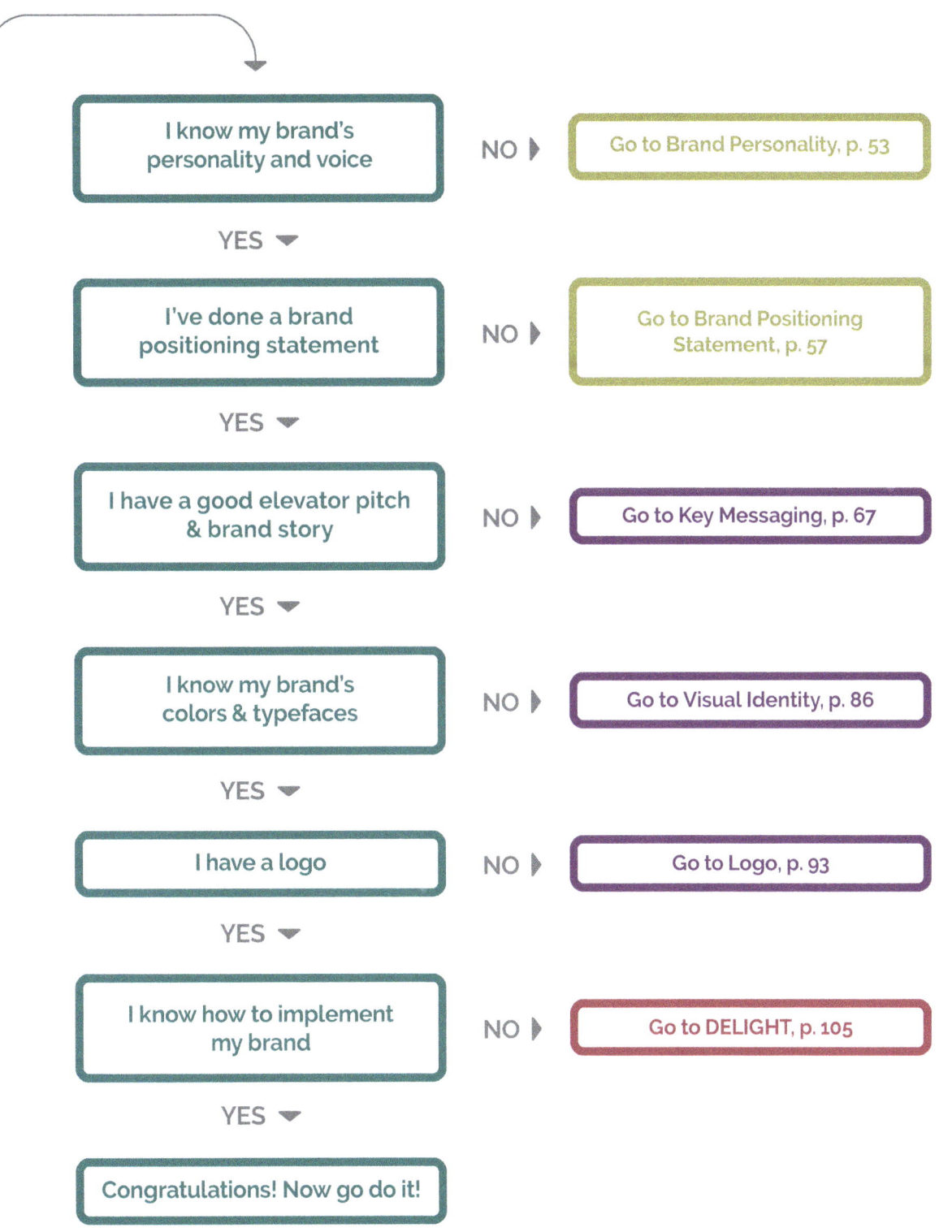

NOTES

Use this space to jot down, sketch, doodle, or mindmap your thoughts or to-do items. You'll find similar Notes pages at the end of each chapter.

PART 2:
DISCOVER

2. DISCOVER

YOU: Who you are and what you want
- What do you desire to do creatively?
- What distinguishes you (how are you different)?
- What do you believe (values) and why do you exist (purpose)?

THEM: Who they are and what they want
- Understanding your favorite fan
- Understanding their drives and desires
- Listening to them

DISCOVER: YOU

To discover is to find out something you didn't know before—about you or your audiences. *For you, it means discovering your creative identity*: who you are and what you want as a creative. *For your audiences, it means discovering who they are and what they want.*

Here in DISCOVER: YOU, we'll focus on your creative identity—your drives and distinctives, what motivates and makes you different. Then, in DISCOVER: THEM, we'll look at how you discover what matters to your audience. Before we dive in, however, it's time for—wait for it—a quiz!

"Yikes!" you may be thinking. "Nobody told me I'd be tested on any of this." But this quiz is for you alone. One of the best ways to learn a new subject is to test yourself on it *before* you start studying. Backwards, I know. But it works. So here goes. Take your best shot at these:

1. **How would you describe what you do** (as it applies to your creative brand)? _____

2. **What three words come to mind when you think about your brand?** _____

3. **Who, in your opinion, would love your brand the most?** _____

4. **What's the most valuable thing your brand provides** (or could provide) to that person or people? Think of both what it does for them and how it makes them feel. _____

5. **What does/could your brand do better than any other similar brand?** _____

Five questions. How hard was that?

Now it's time to understand your motivations for creating because these will reveal your longings or desires, which, in turn, reveal why you're making the things you're making. Getting clear on this has personal benefits, but it will also help you clarify later what makes your brand distinctive. Here goes …

Tip

WHY THIS MATTERS

Many creative people aren't clear about what they want. At least not specifically. They may be unsure of what project to do next or which career direction to follow. My advice? Just keep moving forward. You can start by understanding as much as you can about your desires through the following exercises, then just experiment and pursue what interests you most. I've found that approach to be the surest way to get unstuck and also to build your brand.

DESIRE

Even though your creative brand is about more than just you, it starts with and reflects you to a remarkable degree. Therefore, the clearer you are about who you are and why you're doing what you do, the easier it will be to incorporate more of the authentic you into your brand. And the more effective your brand will be at connecting with others. So let's look at what you love and why.

DESIRE: THE LISTS OF FIVE

- List your **five favorite movies**: _____
_____
_____
_____

- List your **five favorite books**: _____
_____
_____
_____

- List **five best compliments** you've ever received: _____
_____
_____
_____

- List **five favorite experiences** playing as a child: _____
_____
_____
_____

- List **five moments when you behaved or created at your best:**
_____
_____
_____

FIND THE THREAD

Reflect on the patterns or commonalties between your Lists of Five answers. There's usually an overt connection and then something much deeper. It's the latter you want to uncover.

Done? Now look for the patterns or connecting threads between each item in each set (e.g., what do all the movies have in common? The books? Your favorite play experiences?). The purpose is to better understand you, your interests, desires, and even skills and values. This may seem unrelated to your brand, but it will inform the exercises to come.

For example, I realized that in some of my favorite movies, the heroes have strong moral compasses but other characters don't see that (e.g., *The Big Country* or *The*

Mission). In others, there's a strong but quirky family connection (e.g., *The Fantastic Mr. Fox, The Incredibles, Extremely Loud and Incredibly Close*).

Knowing that helps me realize my brand will likely emphasize positive values and relationships. There's much more I can take away from this, but I'll keep that private since, as you'll find, this exercise can be quite personal and revealing.

So take a moment to write down any thoughts on themes, patterns or insights that come to mind from your lists: ___
_____
_____
_____

DESIRE: DREAMS AND GOALS

The Lists of Five is an indirect way to connect you to your dreams and desires. Now let's be more direct. You can ponder the following questions at length, but I find it is best done if you don't overthink them and just write your first answer. Ready? Here we go:

- **What do you long to try creatively or what have you always wanted to do that you haven't done yet?** No clarifications here. Just whatever comes to mind: _____
_____
_____
_____
_____

- **What do you hope to accomplish with your creative work**? Is it self-expression or changing the world? Or likely, somewhere in between? _____
_____
_____
_____
_____

- **What is your favorite medium or genre to work in?** Medium is the form or material you use. For painters, it could be oil, acrylic, watercolor, etc. For writers it could be genre (fiction, nonfiction, poetry, etc.) or subgenre (SciFi, Romance, Mystery, etc.). This is a vital question because it turns out medium has the strongest

tie to motivation. Many creatives only take off when they find the right medium for them. _____
_____
_____

- **What projects do you want to work on most?** Known projects (ones you've already planned or considered)? Dream Projects? Finding what interests you most is the key to getting started and sticking to a project since, as a creative, you likely have many ideas. Which is the most exciting to you *right now?* _____
_____
_____

- **Which project seems to be in most demand?** If you have multiple creative interests, then looking at what your audience wants most can be the tiebreaker for you. Here's a way to further prioritize what to work on now:

DREAMS AND GOALS

Prioritize what you should do by finding those projects that are both easiest to accomplish and have the greatest value

What are your top three priorities right now?

> The medium in which you choose to work has a strong correlation to motivation. For example, don't just try throwing bowls in clay. Try handbuilding them, carving them in wood, or using a 3D printer. You won't know your preferred medium unless you try many.

Let's try a few more:

- **What would you love for people to say about you at your funeral?** Sounds morbid, but it helps connect what you're doing to your long-term goals. _____
_____
_____

- **What does success look like for you?** How will you measure your success or know you've reached it? How you measure success—money, fame, satisfaction, the difference you make, etc.—will affect your brand. _____

_____
_____
_____
_____

- **What's keeping you from achieving your goals right now?** These roadblocks could be: resource challenges (time, money, help from others); mindset blocks ("I'm not good enough," "This is too hard" "I don't know what I'm doing"); or actual lack of skill, experience or knowledge. Identifying roadblocks helps you know where to focus to overcome these challenges. _____
_____
_____
_____
_____

That's it in terms of your desires. Now let's look at what makes you distinctive.

DISTINCTION

DISTINCTION: PERSONALITY

Every brand, just like each person, has a distinct personality. Another benefit of a creative brand over a personal brand is that *your brand's personality can be slightly different (but congruent) with your own.* For example, I, personally, may be a bit more snarky than my creative brand of Explore Your Worlds. For that brand, I'll be intentionally more encouraging in my writing than I might in my day-to-day interactions as a person.

Your personality guides your brand's voice. This is critical because *your voice is how you say something and that, in today's crowded market, matters as much or more than what you say.*

To figureced out your brand personality, start with traits others have told you about your own personality, then select or modify the ones that you think fit best for your creative brand. You want to make a list of five to seven personality traits for your brand. And if you need some help, here's a starting list of traits.

DESIRE AND DISTINCTION

We begin the move from your internal creative identity to your external creative brand when we move from what you love to do (Desire) to what makes you stand out (Distinction). As you begin this section on Distinction, approach it with your audience in mind more than you have in the Desire section.

You want to create your work based on Desire, what interests you most. Asking your audience what to do or chasing the market rarely produces great work. But when it comes to marketing that work, you need to be able to communicate your Distinction so that new audiences can understand your relevance to them.

accessible	active	adaptable	adventurous	affable
affectionate	agreeable	alert	aligned	ambitious
ambiguous	articulate	balanced	bold	bright
brave	calm	capable	captivating	careful
caring	charming	cheerful	clever	collaborative
considerate	compassionate	competitive	confident	connected
cool	courageous	courteous	creative	curious
daring	decent	decisive	dependable	determined
dignified	diligent	diplomatic	dynamic	eager

You can find a more complete list on the worksheets at BrandSomethingBeautiful.com.

My brand personality traits are:

_____
_____
_____
_____
_____
_____
_____

DISTINCTION: CREDIBILITY AND DIFFERENCE

Now let's turn from your personality and answer the question of "Why you?" ***Why would someone buy something from you or trust you for answers or solutions to their need?*** This credibility could relate to your skills, education, experience, awards, testimonials from others, number of sales, other social proof points such as number of followers, etc. Jot down as many reasons as you can to answer the "Why you?" question, then circle the top five reasons you are (or could become) THE expert on your chosen subject.

For artists, you may not care about being the "expert" (something more critical to a personal brand) but your proof points could relate to your distinguishing use of color, how you integrate abstract and representational elements, the other artists with whom you've collaborated, etc. Ordinary people buy art because they love a particular piece. Collectors buy art based on the context that surrounds the artist and

THE VALUE OF SOCIAL PROOF

Social proof are markers of credibility bestowed by others: degrees, awards, followers, years in the market, and other public recognition. Some writers I know enter competitions primarily so they can use the phrase "award-winning author" before their name. That may sound like vanity, but they recognize it is a small social proof that provides credibility even if potential readers never bother to check what award the writer won. Don't underestimate how much social proof markers can help.

that piece. And that context includes all these proof points, including your unique creative identity.

List five proof points for you and your work:

_____
_____
_____
_____
_____

Now, let's look at *what makes you different from others and answer, "Why you over them?"* Even if you're not asking this to be competitive in the market, it's still vital to be able to articulate your distinctives and help prospects differentiate you. Some of your differences may be the same as your proof points. Maybe, as a musician, it's your distinct blend of Indian tonality with Eastern European folk songs that work for the beats of EDM tracks. Or maybe it is your technique as a sculptor, the locations in which you perform as a performance artist, or your subject as a writer (e.g., you focus on emerging technology from unusual sources).

It doesn't help to compare yourself to the top creators in your field, but you can learn from them. For example, take screenwriter, playwright, and director Aaron Sorkin. Don't compare yourself to him and what he's done as the writer-creator of *The West Wing* and *The Newsroom* or his screenplays for *A Few Good Men*, *Moneyball*, or *The Social Network* (for which he won an Academy Award). Instead, note how he's differentiated his work through distinctives such as snappy dialogue, intelligent characters, contemporary issues, or sharp humor.

As with most of these exercises, *there's no one right answer.* The point is to help you determine how you're distinctive in the market. Here goes.

List five distinctives about you or your work:

_____
_____
_____
_____
_____

WHY YOU?

I've heard too many creatives give me generic answers for how they're different or why someone should buy their work. And then they wonder why their work doesn't sell well. The better your answers here, the easier it will be later in crafting your brand positioning statement and even your key messaging. Take time to answer the "Why you?" question.

DISTINCTION: CATEGORY

Walk into a grocery story and you'll find all the products organized by their category: produce, dairy, meat, detergent, etc. *Categories help customers find things—including us as creatives.* Category as a concept can get messy and detailed with sub-categories and fancy terms like brand architecture. But to keep it simple here, let's focus on your category and your specialty.

If you want the shortcut approach to defining your category, think of how you'd answer the question, "What do you do?" when asked by a stranger about your creative work. "I'm a(n) _____" (artist, writer, musician, programmer, etc.) can get you pretty close to what your category is, at least for our purposes here.

But let's go one step further with specialty. *Specialty is what distinguishes you in your category.* Let's say you're an architect. Your widest category is that: architect. But your specialty might be in designing LEED-certified tiny homes with modernist sensibilities. If you're a composer, maybe your specialty is harmonious atonality. A graphic designer? Your specialty could range from woodcut illustrations to avatar development to having an uncanny knack for nailing logo design on the first round. There may be millions of graphic designers (the top-level category) but only you have a proven record of understanding any client's brand so intuitively that you can translate that into a killer logo every time (your specialty).

Now keep in mind, using that example, you may still produce annual reports, landing pages, packaging, posters, etc. But your specialty isn't just logo design. It's uncannily fast and on-target logo design.

If this exercise feels eerily similar to the last two on proof points and differences, that's because your specialty *is* one of your differences and perhaps one of your proof points. The intent here is to get a general sense of your top-level category and then one or a few of your specialties. We'll learn how to talk about these in an integrated fashion later in the DEFINE and DESIGN stages, but for now, the purpose of clarifying your category and specialty is just another way to help you see how you can stand out from the crowd.

Tip

KEEP IT SIMPLE

Don't overthink your category or even your specialty. Reflect on the writers, actors, singers, artists, or even entrepreneurs that you admire. You likely consider their category only as a starting point. It's their brand identity—what we'll get to in the DEFINE section—that matters most.

However, I know that many multi-hyphenated creatives (you know, the composer-designer-producer-chef types) struggle with which aspect of their creative work to emphasize. Thus, I've added a section in the Appendix on what, in the branding world, we call Brand Architecture. If you have multiple, different audiences, you may need more than one brand, so check out the Appendix.

However, for most creatives, one brand is enough. Keep it simple, nail that brand, and you can expand to more over time if you need to.

So give this one a try as well. List your category and specialty: _____
_____
_____

DISTINCTION: COMPETITION

So far, we've focused mostly on you. Now we turn to how to understand your distinctive approach within the marketplace. Your first step is to **find five other brands in the same category as yours that come close to what you offer**. You're not limited to just five (simply add rows). But try to get at least five to have a good sense of what is out there. If you're an author, you've likely had to do this in your book proposal by finding "comps"—other books similar to yours. In book proposals, you don't want any comps that are over two years old. The same applies here. Only focus on the works of "competitors" that are recent.

Whatever your field or medium, there will be others doing similar work. If there isn't, that means you're either a genius but ahead of your time (and thus the market may not be ready for your work), or you're creating a product no one wants. That can sound harsh, but your goal isn't to come up with a brand-new category, at least not when you're getting started. Your goal is to be close enough to others in your field, but different enough to stand out. Suzanne Collins didn't invent the genre of a dystopian future. But with *The Hunger Games* she differentiated herself through her characters, plot, etc.

If you're not sure where to find competitors, you can start with a basic Google search on your topic or area of interest, but I'm finding Google's Gemini, ChatGPT, or Claude.ai gives me better results. Use a search term or prompt such as "best sites for _____ (artists, watercolor painters, oil painters, writers, calligraphers, cartographers, gallery owners, etc.)." Or, try a prompt like, "I'm a reporter doing a story on _____(artists in the field of X, writers of Y, performers focusing on these types of performances, etc.). Please provide ten examples of others doing similar work along with samples of that work, where they operate, how long they've been doing this, and how popular they are." If the results aren't exactly ones in

 Resource

BRAND ARCHETYPES

You may have heard about archetypes such as The Ruler, The Sage, The Outlaw, The Creator, etc. These can be helpful for some creatives in determining their brands or, specifically, helping them with their category. So if you want more information on brand archetypes, go to BrandSomethingBeautiful.com for a list of additional resources on archetypes and other creative branding tools.

Tip

WHY KNOWING YOUR COMPETITORS MATTERS

You're not doing this to compare yourself to others. That's always a recipe for angst. You're looking instead to get specific ideas on how to position your own work in ways that resonate with your audience. Phrases, keywords, visual approaches—see what's out there not to copy, but to learn what's working.

your field, add in some of your proof points, differences, or specialties into your prompt to get results closer to you and your work.

One of my favorite tools, if you're an author, is Publisher Rocket (www.publisherrocket.com) which not only shows you other books in your category but also the keywords they use and their ranking on Amazon.

There's really no wrong way to do this, but many artists and creatives don't take the time to see what else is out there. So just get started with some basic search terms and you'll find additional resources that will point you toward others.

Let's start with your five comparison brands. *List those (individuals or companies) who produce work most like yours.* It can help to note their website or social handles as well for easier future reference.

My five top competitors are:

_____
_____
_____
_____
_____

Competitor Name	Similarities	Differences	Dislikes	Likes
1:				
2:				
3:				
4:				
5:				

Now comes the fun part: For each "competitor," list how you're similar and how you're different. Then add notes on what you like and dislike about each. These can be your preferences regarding how the competitor presents their brand on their website or in social media, the language they use, the personality they present, or whatever grabs you. For example, you may like the colors of one, the way their online gallery works for another, the playful language of yet another, the freebies provided, etc. Note whatever will be helpful to you.

For the "dislikes" box, these will be elements you want to make sure you avoid in your own brand or website like "confusing explanation of services" or "hard to see close-ups of artwork." In short, your similarities and differences are notes about the brand itself, and your likes and dislikes are about how they present their brand. Add columns for additional criteria that are important to you, such as benefits they offer, specialty, location, attitude (tone and voice) or whatever helps you. Take some time now to fill out your version of the table.

After you've completed the table, summarize your thoughts about how you're different from any of them. You may be similar in some areas (e.g., you both write speculative fiction), but your difference may be in the time or location where your novels take place. So, ask yourself, *"How am I (or really, how is my work) different?"* More importantly, *how is that difference something that might matter to your audiences?*

GET MORE ONLINE

An editable version of this table and the other forms shown here are available to you within the worksheets at BrandSomethingBeautiful.com.

My brand stands out from the competition in the following ways:

- _____
- _____
- _____
- _____

DISTINCTION: VALUES & PURPOSE

Now you know more about you and your competition, it's time to complete this "For You" section with **two vital summary concepts: your values (beliefs) and your** *purpose (why you exist)*. I've spent decades helping organizations work on their mission and vision statements, most of which get debated, rehashed, and ultimately ignored. But I've found this simple format to be more helpful:

I/we believe_____
_____.

I/we exist to_____
_____.

The examples on the right should help you see how it is used.

The "believe" part is your way to convey your highest value for your brand. With Western Union (see the next page examples), they cheated a bit on the format but still conveyed what they believe. ***The "exist to" part becomes an expression of your purpose***, what you hope to achieve through your creative brand. I've added my own brand, Explore Your Worlds to show that for this exercise, you can be rather lofty because this gets at your "why" and guides the more tactical elements of your brand such as medium, technique, etc. Be aspirational about what you truly value or believe and your reason for creating. And on a more prosaic note, you can replace "I" with "we" if your brand represents more than one person, or if you're a big fan of *The Crown* and you like using the royal "we."

Now it's your turn. Fill in the blanks for your creative brand:

I/we believe: _____
_____
_____

I/we exist to: _____
_____
_____

CONGRATULATIONS!

You've finished the "For You" part of the DISCOVER phase of the branding process. Now it is time to turn from you to them and discover, or at least record and organize, some key insights about your audience.

DO THIS

This simple exercise of "believe and exist to" statements is far more helpful than traditional mission or purpose statements. This approach tends to be more inspirational and aspirational and often provides more compelling language than a typical mission statement. You'll use the results of this many times later on in your brand and messaging.

NIKE
- We believe: If you have a body, you're an athlete.
- We exist to: Outfit the athlete in every one of us.

STARBUCKS
- We believe: Coffee has the power to create community.
- We exist to: Inspire and nurture the human spirit one person, one cup, one neighborhood at a time.

APPLE
- We believe: There is a creative genius in everyone.
- We exist to: Ignite people's creativity through technology.

HALLMARK
- We believe: An emotionally connected world is a better world.
- We exist to: Help people create genuine connections in moments that matter.

WESTERN UNION
- We believe in people all over the world who are on the move to pursue a better life.
- We exist to: Move money anytime and anywhere so people can pursue their dreams.

EXPLORE YOUR WORLDS
- We believe: There's more to life than most people realize.
- We exist to: Help people discover and live out that more.

DISCOVER: THEM

In his book, *The Practice,* marketing guru Seth Godin notes that if your creative work isn't selling, it's likely for one of three reasons:

1. *It's the wrong audience.* You're trying to sell sci-fi to romance fans, thinking it will work because there's a romance scene wedged in between the spaceship battles.

2. *It's the right audience but the wrong timing.* You're making Art Deco furniture when the market wants Mid-century Modern.

3. *Your craft isn't sufficient.* Your work isn't of the same or better quality as others in your field.

You address the last point by practicing and committing to excellence. But the first two points are all about audience. Thus, **if you want to sell your creative work, it means understanding your audience well.** All the next steps in building your brand will be based on a good—hopefully even great—understanding of your audience.

The easiest way to do this is to create a persona of your favorite fan. This is an avatar or character that represents the one person or a collective of people who love your work the most. Because each brand may have very different audiences, in the worksheets found at Brand-SomethingBeautiful.com, you can create an image (draw or use a photo) that looks more like your favorite fan than the illustration here.

It's important you focus on a narrow audience here because if you think that "everyone" is a possible customer or client, then really, that means no one is. No creative work will appeal to everyone, so try to be as specific as possible. If you truly do have two or more very distinctive audiences, you can make a separate persona for each. And if they are really that different, you may need a separate brand for each. In the Appendix, I address how to apply this if you have multiple brands. For now, try to focus on your primary audience and fill in the blanks here for your favorite fan.

DO THIS

This whole section is vital since knowing your audience is one of the most important and least practiced parts of the creative brand. If you're only guessing at who might love your work, you'll waste a lot of time, money, and effort chasing the wrong target.

A paradox here is that *the more niche you go, the more you're likely to sell.*

PERSONA
(YOUR FAVORITE FAN)

NAME: _____
EDUCATION: _____
AGE: _____ STATUS: _____
APPEARANCE & PERSONALITY: _____

NEEDS
(WHAT PROBLEMS ARE THEY TRYING TO SOLVE?)

BELIEFS
(WHAT DO THEY VALUE?)

MOTIVATIONS
(WHAT INSPIRES THEM?)

YOUR RESPONSE

WHAT ONE INSIGHT WOULD BE MOST HELPFUL TO THEM?

HOW CAN I HELP THEM SOLVE THEIR PROBLEMS?

WHAT RESOURCES COULD I PROVIDE TO HELP THEM MOST RIGHT NOW?

DESIRES
(WHAT DO THEY WANT?)

DISLIKES
(WHAT DON'T THEY WANT?)

INSPIRATION
(WHERE DO THEY GO FOR NEW IDEAS?)

SOLUTIONS
(WHERE DO THEY GO TO MEET THEIR NEEDS?)

BELIEFS OVER STATS

Your tribe or target audience likely shares values and interests more than demographics like income or education. Unless your product is for expectant mothers or retirees, your audience may have more in common based on passion than on typical demographics such as age, ethnicity, location, etc. Many personas get built around demographic stats. The most effective, however, focus more on shared interests, needs, and motivations.

USE THEIR WORDS

Once you know the needs of your audience, think through the keywords they'd use to search for your work online. Knowing their search terms can guide your own brand language in the DEFINE phase.

SUMMARY THOUGHTS ON YOUR AUDIENCE

This takes time, but hopefully you realize just how much or how little you know about your primary audience. If any of these questions are hard to answer, just ask your favorite fan. Novel idea, I know. But it's amazing how many people try to build their brands and never have met or at least spoken with someone in their target audience. They instead guess at the answers and—big surprise—those answers reflect the perspectives of the creator, not their audience. Go to events where your audience hangs out. Do an online survey. Bring up some of these questions in a Facebook group with your audience. Have coffee with your favorite fan.

If you connect with your audience directly, consider asking them the same questions that started this whole module on DISCOVER but framed from their perspective:

1. **How would you describe what I do (as it applies to your creative brand)?**
2. **What three words come to mind when you think about my brand?**
3. **Who, in your opinion, would love my brand the most?**
4. **What's the most valuable thing my brand provides?**
5. **What does my brand do better than a similar brand?**

Then, compare your answers with theirs.

Notice how you're not asking them, "What should I make?" Your goal is to understand their needs, not take their advice creatively. Audiences are notorious for saying they want one thing then buying the opposite. They often don't know what they want until they see it. You don't want the market to dictate what you make, but your audience's needs should inform your creative considerations. See the difference?

The benefit of really getting to know your audience is that you'll create work with their needs in mind and better target all your marketing efforts later. You'll also experience profound relief by knowing more about how your audience thinks, what they like, what words they use, and what they need. It makes the whole process easier and will change how you think about marketing and sales.

If you do this work now, you won't feel like you're either being pushy in selling something people don't want, or doing ads to an amorphous mass audience and just hoping something might catch on. Instead, you'll begin to realize just how valuable your work can be to them and how much they'll appreciate knowing about it. While this may take you some time to work through, it not only will save you weeks or even months of time and a lot of emotional energy down the road, it will make you feel better about your work and the marketing and selling of that work.

SUMMARY OF THE BOOK SO FAR

Let's take stock of what you've done to this point. So far you've:

- Understood what a brand is and what makes a creative brand different.

- Realized how vital it is to make an emotional connection with your audiences and how you as a person are more than your brand.

- Understood that the creator's branding process involves the four stages of DISCOVER, DEFINE, DESIGN, and DELIGHT.

- Worked through the DISCOVER stage by:
  - ☑ Exploring your desires, dreams, and goals.
  - ☑ Exploring your distinctives in the areas of personality, credibility, difference, and category.
  - ☑ Understanding who your competitors are and how you differ from them.
  - ☑ Creating your believe/exist statements to articulate your values and purpose.
  - ☑ Doing a deep dive into your target audience and what they want and need.

Corporations may take months and pay hundreds of thousands or even millions of dollars to do what you have just done. So take a moment to congratulate yourself on all the insights you've gained and progress you've made. Now that you've made all these important discoveries about you and your audience, it's time to do something with all this by moving to the next step where you will DEFINE your brand.

1,000 TRUE FANS

Back in 2008, *Wired* magazine co-founder Kevin Kelly introduced the idea of 1,000 True Fans. You don't need millions of fans to succeed, just 1,000 people who love your work so much, they will pay, say $100/year for it. That's $100,000 of income each year. But it all starts with knowing who they are and what they value.

NOTES

PART 3:
DEFINE

DEFINE *YOUR BRAND IDENTITY*

Your Big Idea ▶ Your Secret Sauce ▶ Your Personality and Voice ▶

▶ Your offerings and how you make people feel ▶ Your Role ▶ Your Positioning ▶ Your Special Resource

Congratulations! ! You've made it to the DEFINE section, where you'll *craft your brand identity*. Keep in mind that this brand identity is primarily internal. Everything you've done in DISCOVER serves as a foundation for this brand identity, and the brand identity then serves as a foundation for all your external messaging, design, and marketing.

As noted earlier, you can think of your brand identity as the strategy for (or even a summary of) how to position your creative work. Or, think of it as similar to your own personal identity in how it represents who you are. It will make more sense as we go, so hang in there if any terms aren't clear now.

We'll cover the external aspects of your brand (your verbal and visual elements) later in the DESIGN section. But those won't work very well unless you build these internal elements first. Here's an overview of all these pieces:

BRAND IDENTITY

WHAT'S YOUR BIG IDEA?
Essence—The summary concept that connects and reflects the unique way you do your work

WHAT'S YOUR WHY?
Purpose—The reason you do what you do

INTERNAL

WHO YOU ARE

What are your unique attributes?
Characteristics—Qualities that differentiate you and clarify your essence

How do you act?
Personality Traits—What the brand would be like if it were a person

Where do you fit in the marketplace?
Positioning Statement—How you position yourself vis-a-vis others

HOW YOU ACT:
Brand Behaviors

WHAT YOU OFFER

What promise can you keep?
Promise—What your audiences get from you

What benefits do you provide?
Value Proposition—Core offering: functional, emotional, and self-expressive benefits

How do you make them feel?
Primary Emotional Benefit—What you want audiences to feel after engaging with you

HOW YOU RELATE:
Relational Metaphor

EXTERNAL

WHAT YOU SAY:
Key Messaging

HOW YOU SPEAK:
Voice and Tone

HOW YOU LOOK:
Visual Identity

To make this even easier for you to picture, here's a preview of coming attractions, an example using my brand Explore Your Worlds to show you how the brand identity fits together. I'll explain all the elements later, but if you're like me, it's nice to have a mental model up front of your destination. Here goes ...

EXPLORE YOUR WORLDS BRAND IDENTITY

- **What's the big idea or guiding principle of the brand** (essence)?
  - ▷ *Discover and Create*
- **What promise do you make to your audience** (brand promise, a synthesis of the benefits you provide)?
  - ▷ *(To help them) travel creatively and create adventurously*
- **What do you provide?** (core offerings):
  - ▷ *Articles, blog posts, quizzes, free ebooks and other digital resources, photographs, books, courses, speaking engagements, coaching, consulting*
- **What does the brand do for your audience** (functional benefits)?
  - ▷ *Offers inspiring and informative content*
  - ▷ *Builds their capacity (and desire) to travel and create*
  - ▷ *Helps them think about travel and creativity in new ways*
  - ▷ *Connects travel and creativity to what they value most in life*
  - ▷ *Provides real-world examples and permission*
- **How does the brand make them feel** (emotional benefits)?
  - ▷ *Adventurous*
  - ▷ *Competent and confident*
  - ▷ *Freer to pursue what interests them*
  - ▷ *Inspired and excited to try/make new things*

- ▷ *Able to explore new possibilities*
- **Which of these is the most important for them to feel** (top emotional benefit)?
    - ▷ *Inspired and capable*
- **How does the brand make them see themselves** (self-expressive benefits)?
    - ▷ *Adventurous, more creative and capable*
- **What are the key distinctives of the brand** (brand attributes)?
    - ▷ *__Unlikely Synthesis__: Bringing together diverse and often unexpected perspectives*
    - ▷ *__The Pursuit of MORE:__ Connecting one's internal and external worlds*
    - ▷ *__Relentless Curiosity:__ Seeking wonder, embracing mystery, and maintaining openness*
    - ▷ *__Gracious Intentionality:__ Few great things come about without effort, but it is always better to woo and compel than to lecture*
    - ▷ *__Personal yet Shared:__ In art and travel, discover the ways and places that matter most to you and you will discover what matters to others*
- **How does the brand sound** (your voice characteristics)?
    - ▷ *__Encouraging:__ Compassionate, empathetic, and enthusiastic*
    - ▷ *__Practical__: Helpful, honest/authentic, realistic*
    - ▷ *__Humble:__ Self-effacing, humorous, and willing to ask "stupid" questions*
    - ▷ *__Experienced:__ Practiced yet open, professional yet fun, knowledgeable yet with childlike wonder*
- **How do I summarize all this into one statement** (brand positioning statement)?
    - ▷ *For people who love to journey and to make, Explore Your Worlds is the experienced guide to help them travel creatively and create adventurously through its inspiring content, supportive approach, and unexpected ways to discover more.*

INTERNAL VS. EXTERNAL

While what you define here in your brand identity ultimately will undergird all your external communications, the concepts themselves are internal. Don't waste time wordsmithing each of these for your audiences. That comes later. For your brand identity, just get the ideas down so that you understand them and can build on them later.

You may not yet grasp what each of these components means, but you can probably see how the work you've already done comes into play. You likely don't have an essence (big idea) statement yet, but you may be close. You have your personality traits. And that work on target audience and category will inform the positioning statement. By taking the time to dive deep into your audience, you already know what they want and need. So now, let's explore each element starting with the most important: your big idea, AKA your brand essence.

BRAND ESSENCE

Your essence is your big idea summarized into a small phrase (only one to four or five words). I won't lie: this is the hardest part of your brand to develop because it needs to pack a big punch in few words. The essence is the key principle behind all that you do and the concept that guides you and keeps your brand consistent and on track. It's the connecting thread that unites or at least weaves its way through all your creative work—the fundamental nature, soul, or deepest quality of your brand.

Maybe it is the one trait you're most known for. Maybe it is the heart of your creative identity or your singular way of seeing the world. Perhaps it summarizes what you uncovered in your Lists of Five exercises (page 18) or even your Purpose/Exist to statement (page 28). It is a concept, an internal one, and not a tagline or slogan. Because you're more used to taglines, e.g., Nike's "Just do it," you will likely gravitate in that direction. Don't. "Optimal athletic performance," Nike's essence, isn't as sexy. But it isn't meant to be. ***The tagline derives from the essence.*** You start with the internal essence concept first and then find external expressions of it later in the DESIGN phase.

Let's start by going back to your list of your credibility or differences, your unique take on your work (page 23). Is there a word or short phrase that comes out of that exercise that defines your big idea or essence? Be specific. If you're a painter, don't say "Color" unless you can define how you approach color differently. If you're a writer, don't say "Romance" because that's a genre, not your essence. If you write romance novels, what's your big idea behind those?

DO THIS

The essence is the most important part of your brand and the missing piece in most creative and even organizational brands. It is also, in most cases, the hardest part, so hang in there and realize it will come. Just don't settle for something that sounds like a tagline rather than the true heart of your brand.

Maybe it is something like "Loving the Unlovable" because you always make your protagonist someone that others look down on. Or maybe your essence is "Hopeful Pursuit" because everything you write reflects an optimistic viewpoint, something your audiences prefer.

That last part is key: *Your essence has to offer a benefit, even if only implied, to your audience.* Thus, let's say that your List of Five books revealed you love stories where the protagonist goes through an unusual struggle (that is different than the typical hero's journey narrative). That might clue you in that your brand will be iconoclastic, non-traditional, or simply surprising. And likely, you'll appeal to an audience that appreciates those same factors. If your favorite movies list revealed that you root for the underdog, your essence may be something like "championing the underdog" or "overcoming." With an essence of "overcoming," everything you then do for your brand will reflect that grit, determination, and the hope of defying the odds. You'll appeal to readers who like movies such as *Rudy*, or who root for Frodo in *The Lord of the Rings*, or who long for Jane Eyre to find happiness.

For your essence, it helps to target the big idea or soul notion that, in the best case, has emotional resonance with you and your audiences and covers more than the theme of just one or a few of your works. Earlier, you saw Hallmark's believe/exist statement: "We believe an emotionally connected world is a better world. We exist to help people create genuine connections in moments that matter." It ties to their essence of "Caring Shared." Note how there's nothing in the essence related to greeting cards or any of their products. The essence is strictly conceptual but, as we've seen, emotionally resonant as well. On its own, "Caring Shared" could be the essence of a florist, co-op, or even Airbnb. Thus, your essence doesn't have to convey your distinctiveness completely. Your category combined with your Characteristics (we'll get to those soon) will do that. But a *great essence makes everything else about the brand suddenly clearer.*

The essence describes the feeling you want the brand to evoke. That feeling can be an emotion (e.g., **Subaru and "love"**) or an intangible sense (**"adventure" for Jeep** or even

Your essence is a big idea, not a narrow description. An internal construct, not an external tagline.

essence

noun

1. The intrinsic or indispensable quality or qualities that serve to characterize or identify something.

   "The essence of democracy is the freedom to choose."

2. The inherent, unchanging nature of a thing or class of things.

3. The most important part or aspect of something.

   "The essence of her argument is that the policy is wrongheaded."

—The American Heritage Dictionary

GO FOR THE HEART

The essence of Airbnb is "Belonging." Every person longs to belong. Airbnb's essence therefore has baked-in emotional qualities. Plus, you'll note that Airbnb's essence doesn't focus on functional aspects of apartments. Their essence goes to the heart of what they offer—both to guests who want to "belong" to a local neighborhood, and to hosts who "belong" to an insider's circle through participating with Airbnb.

FREEDOM

When you learn that Harley Davidson's essence is "Freedom," you see the brand in a whole new way. Your experience of riding a Harley is different, as a result, from riding another motorcycle.

"community" for Starbucks). Or perhaps a key product benefit that rises to the level of dominant positioning (*"safety" for Volvo*). It can be a grounded aspiration of intent (*"learning through creative play" for LEGO*) or almost a self-expressive benefit (meaning it changes how the audience sees themselves) as in *"optimal athletic performance" as we saw, for Nike.* They all seem intuitive once you know the brands, because the brands have grown into and around these essences.

For individuals or small businesses in the creative realm, the approach is no different. Some essence examples from various artists and creatives I know include "Encouraging Travel" for a writer who helps people new to the travel experience, and "Culture" for a memoirist whose stories all deal with crossing cultures.

Key to all these is that **the essence only has to make sense to you**. Eventually, in the DESIGN phase, you'll translate it into external expressions such as your key messaging and copy. But using the example of the memoirist's "Culture," if you don't know the context and the work of that particular writer, the word "culture" alone won't make sense. But if you do know their work, then you can see why "culture" is a great connecting thread. Same with the essence of "Reconciliation" for a visual artist whose work may never overtly illustrate the term, but for whom reconciliation is an internal motivation in everything he does.

Essences are usually best kept broad and even intangible. Harley Davidson isn't about "Riding Freedom" or "Freedom of the Open Road." Those would limit the brand. Volvo's essence of "Safety" isn't "safe automobiles" because they also make truck engines and other products. Your essence is a big idea, not a narrow description.

Sometimes your essence can be more focused, an articulation of your distinctive. For example, I worked with a graphic designer who can take any concept, even abstract ones, and come up with visuals to convey the idea. For him, we decided his category wasn't just graphic design. It was "visual translation." That then became his essence as well. See how this category (or specialty in the graphic design category) can be used to define the heart of all that he does? It's turned out to be his superpower (as it relates to his creative work), his category, and his essence.

SOME AIDS TO CRAFTING AN ESSENCE

One little trick I often use with clients is to add a dual meaning to their essence by finding an "-ing" word combined with a noun. An example is "Expanding Possibilities" for an organization that develops written alphabets with people groups around the world who only have a spoken language. The essence has the dual meaning of expanding the possibilities of those they serve, and that those possibilities are themselves expanding or growing in nature. That same double meaning works with the earlier example of "Encouraging Travel."

Another approach is connecting two words that aren't normally combined. A friend of mine runs a counseling center. We realized her brand was about hope, but hope is fairly overused in her circles. But by pairing it with the word "authentic" (also overused on its own), she now has a very distinctive essence: "Authentic Hope."

Sometimes a single powerful concept that you come across in your work will provide the answer. Another nonprofit client works to help those in the inner city build their capacity to overcome various challenges. In a brand workshop, one of their team mentioned a quote from John Perkins, that poverty is essentially a lack of options. That one phrase, combined with the community-oriented nature of their work, led to an essence of "Creating Options Together." This became a powerful rallying cry that worked for single moms struggling to get by, for program leaders trying to build coalitions, and even for donors who saw themselves helping to create options for others. It's one of the few times where an internal essence is powerful enough to be used as a tagline. That can happen, but it is rare that you'll use your essence externally. It's better to concentrate on the concept first, and then find public-facing expressions of it, than to burden yourself with nailing down a killer tagline while struggling to articulate your big idea.

Lest all of this stress you out, know this: ***There is no single right answer.*** You're a creative. You know how that works.

ESSENCE EXAMPLES:

"Caring Shared"—Hallmark

"Magic"—Disney

"Learning through creative play"—LEGO

"Safety"—Volvo

> **Your essence is the connecting thread that unites and guides all you do, the most important or fundamental idea or quality of your brand. Take time to get it right, meaning allow time to reflect on your initial ideas.**

Relax with this. Have fun even. Just give it a shot. Make a list of some options for your essence. Then run them by people who know your brand well and see how they respond. ***Be prepared that most people won't understand what an essence is***. They'll likely be hoping for a tagline. So coach them that this is just an internal concept to get at the heart of your brand. Give them examples like those above, "magic" for Disney, "belonging" for Airbnb, or "learning through creative play" for LEGO. Finally, here are some prompts that may help you come up with essence concepts:

- *What one thing makes your work different from anyone else's in your field?*
- *Is there a word or phrase that stands out in your Believe/Exist statements?*
- *What's your deepest longing for your brand? Summarize that in one to four words.*
- Later, we'll explore the emotions you want your audience to feel. But *is there one primary emotion that your brand induces that could be your big idea?* What emotion does your brand evoke for you?
- *What changes in the life a person who uses your product or service?* Can you summarize that in an inspiring one-to-four-word idea?
- *What's the greatest benefit (emotional or other) that your brand provides?*
- *When people talk to you about your brand, what phrases do you commonly hear?* Are there any surprising expressions you might use?
- *If you paired a key personality trait with a key distinctive about what you do or offer, what would be an interesting combination* (e.g., "Cheerful Realism" or "Brooding Curiosity")?

Now it's your turn. Make a list of up to five possibilities for your essence here:

- _____
- _____

- _____
- _____
- _____

Run your top choices by others, narrow those down to your finalist, and write that down here:

My brand's essence: _____

If you're not sure, that's fine. Hold off and work through the rest of the elements of the brand identity and then return. Often, in doing the other parts, the essence becomes clearer.

And to help with the essence even more, let's now tackle your brand promise.

BRAND PROMISE

Your brand promise is the promise you make and can keep to your audiences. You can't promise to change their lives or even make their lives better with your creative work. That's not up to you. But you can promise to create work that increases the likelihood of that or inspires, educates, entertains, or makes a difference in a particular way.

Sometimes your promise will be the same as your essence. In the two nonprofit examples I mentioned, "creating options together" and "expanding possibilities," both function well as promises. Phrased as a promise, the latter goes something like, "We promise to help you expand possibilities." Can they guarantee that will happen? In their case, yes. Having your own language always creates more possibilities.

As a creative, you may think, "Well, that's great in the social services space, but I just make art." But you don't just make art. Great art transforms people and places. So let's say you are an abstract painter. What promise could you make to your audience? This is why you spent so much time getting to know your audience, so you know what promise matters to them.

What do they want? That's what your promise should be about. "I promise to always be true to myself" may be great for you but not very helpful for your brand or your audience. ***Your promise should be the pinnacle of the benefits that you provide, a statement of the experience they can count on every time they engage with your brand.***

DO THIS

If you're not clear on your promise, you'll be scattered in you messaging. Spend time to find a compelling promise you can deliver.

To help you get there, imagine you're your favorite fan. What experience would you want from your brand? What key benefit would you hope to get?

You can make your promise very serious and business-like. For example, if you're a software developer, you may promise, "Clean code, elegant solutions." ***Or, you can go more fun*** as in this line I heard from a novelist who writes stories that include the protagonist's pet: "The dog doesn't die in the end." Now granted, that is more of a product (or book series) promise than for your brand, but it tells you so much: this author writes with humor, understands her audience, and delivers happy endings. All good elements of a promise for a particular audience.

Your promise can be longer than your essence, but still no more than a short sentence. Walmart does a great job with their promise (which is also their tagline): "Save money. Live better." Unlike other retailers who might make a similar promise, Walmart can back up their claim with data by showing that families can purchase nicer products for less, thus improving their quality of life. That's part of why they added the "live better" element and replaced their old promise of "Always low prices."

To help you get to your promise, go back to the work you've done already. Here are some specific approaches you can try.

- **Meaning**. People derive meaning in many ways: Beauty, Community, Duty, Freedom, Redemption, Security, etc. ***What do you believe provides the greatest meaning to your audience?*** Let's say you chose Community. How might your promise include some way in which you help your audience connect to others or experience deeper relationships? If, say, you're a mural artist, you might promise something like, "Drawing together through art" which has a double meaning, or "Making art as big as your community's dreams." If it helps to keep these from sounding too slogan-like, you can always phrase them as, "I (my brand) promise(s) to _____ _____." And if the promise sounds just too big to be real, you can tone it down with the "help" term such as, "I promise to help make art as big as your community's dreams."

PROMISE TIPS

Focus on:

- How your brand adds meaning to their lives.
- What they will be able to do because of your brand.
- How it meets a felt need.
- How it makes them see themselves.
- How they can overcome challenges because of you.
- A synthesis of your top distinctives.
- Making your promise believable yet inspiring.

- **Accomplishment.** Another aspect of your promise could come from accomplishment. Let's say you're a Marie Kondo-like home and office organizing consultant and you realize that your favorite fan wants to have and maintain a clutter-free home. So your promise might be just that, "A clutter-free home that stays that way." Or you could go more aspirational with, "A clutter-free home for a clutter-free life." That may be an over-promise, but here's the reason it could still work: If your customer follows your instructions and sticks with you over time, they will have a clutter-free life. **You can't control what they do, but you can promise that if they do what you suggest, they'll achieve the promise.** Or use "help" such as, "I help you achieve a clutter-free home and life." That could then translate later into a tagline of "Clutter-free home, clutter-free life."

- **Felt need.** *This is probably the biggest source of inspiration for a promise.* Let's say you're a course designer and your client's biggest felt need includes courses that provide great insights in the least amount of time. If you can deliver on that, again, you can turn that directly into a promise: "More knowledge, less time."

- **Self-expressive benefits.** *These relate to how your favorite fan wants to see themselves.* Perhaps you're an influencer specializing in beauty products and wellness. The obvious self-expressive benefit is that your favorite fan wants to see herself as beautiful. But can you go deeper? What if you could promise them confidence? In that case, your promise might be, "A daily application of confidence" or "I promise to build confidence each day, through each product, for each person." You could shorten this to "Confidence Daily." With that phrase, you start to see how parts of your brand identity, such as the promise here, could be turned into external expressions. "Confidence Daily" could be a strong tagline.

- **Challenges.** Similar to felt need, *what specific challenges does your audience want to overcome?* If you're illustrating children's books, your audiences (likely both the child and the parent) have felt needs of entertainment,

PATAGONIA'S PROMISE

Patagonia offers a believable and motivating promise:

"We provide environmentally responsible adventure." Not just products, but the aspirational results of those products: adventure.

> **What promise can you make that would matter *most* to your audience?**

 **Insight**

KNOWING WHAT YOU PROVIDE

Honestly, I used to rush through this section, particularly for creative brands. After all, the emotional benefits of a song seem clear but what are the functional benefits? But just asking that question changes how you think about your creative work. Realizing that songs can functionally provide a person with company, improve their mood, or serve as pleasant background sound can help you think of new ways to position your brand. So spend time on all these elements. They will prove valuable later when you seek new approaches to marketing you and your creative work.

education, and even, for the book itself, durability or beauty. But the challenge they want to overcome may relate the parent's desire to get their child to read more. You might get toward this with a promise such as, "Stories your child begs you to re-read." Again, that could even be a tagline, as well as a promise.

- **Attributes**. Go back to *your list of proof points or differences that differentiate you from your competitors.* Choose your top three and see if they lead you to a promise statement. For example, if you are a wedding photographer, some key attributes that might emerge could include "inspires original poses, is fun to work with, delivers the results on time, blends in with the guests (isn't obtrusive), and gets great expressions." From those, you might create a promise such as, "Minimizing interruptions to your wedding, maximizing the memories from it." It doesn't cover all the attributes, but hopefully those most important to your audiences. Plus, it summarizes some of them rather than delineates them all.

Your turn. *What's the promise you make—and keep—to your audiences?*

I promise to: _____
_____

CORE OFFERING, FEATURES, AND BENEFITS

Some branding and marketing people call this section the value proposition. I'm not fond of that term because it can be used in so many ways. So rather than use that jargony phrase, let's explore here what you offer (the specific products and services you provide) along with the corresponding features and benefits.

If you did a thorough job of understanding your favorite fan previously, you can apply much of that work here to save you time, especially when you get to the emotional benefits and related issues.

Use the spaces below as the starting point. If you run out of room, just make another list of your own or in your worksheets. Here's what you'll fill out:

1. **What you do or offer:** Make a list of all the primary or core products and services you provide to your audience. This includes things you sell and free things like content, samples, demos, webinars, speaking engagements, or anything else that you make available to your audience. For example, for me, I offer books, website and social media content (blog posts and photos), ebooks and white papers, presentations, webinars, courses, speaking engagements, interviews, articles, coaching, and consultation. However, for the sake of this exercise, I would summarize them all as content and coaching around travel and creativity. You could do this whole exercise for each product, but for our purposes, since we're focusing on your overall brand, try to summarize, either in one category as I did, or in a few if they are distinctive (e.g., I could have divided my offerings into inspiration, products, and coaching/consulting).

2. **Features:** For your offerings, list associated features. An ice maker in a refrigerator is a feature, as is an interactive quiz on your website, or framing and matting included with each print you offer. Similarly, if you made guitars, a feature might be solid wood construction or a built-in amp jack. In my case, features for my brand might include a wealth of free resources, availability in different formats, photographs to support the text, etc.

3. **Benefits**: Beyond features come benefits. These are what the product or service does for the audience. A feature of a hiking book might be waterproofing, but the benefit is that it lets its owner go to more places in all kinds of weather. The benefit of the ice maker is 24/7 cold drinks. Benefits can be broken down into what they do for you (functional benefits), how they make you feel (emotional benefits), and even how they change how you think about yourself or how you see yourself as a result (self-expressive benefits).

With toothpaste, a functional benefit is that it helps prevent cavities or makes your teeth brighter. An emotional benefit is that you feel more confident to smile. A self-expressive benefit is that you see yourself

OFFERINGS:
What you provide (your products or services).

FEATURES:
Key aspects included in the offering.

BENEFITS:
How those features help your audience functionally, emotionally, and in terms of how they see themselves.

as younger or more appealing to others. For the guitar maker, a functional benefit is better resonance from the solid wood construction. An emotional benefit is the joy of experiencing clean high notes and powerful bass notes. A self-expressive benefit might be that guitar owner now sees herself as a more accomplished guitarist and capable of tackling tougher pieces than before. For my brand as a creative, a functional benefit is helpful content that is inspiring, instructive, and digestible in small amounts. An emotional benefit is that my audience feels excited about traveling or creating. A self-expressive benefit is that they see themselves as more adventurous and capable of going to beautiful (but under-the-radar) places and making beautiful things.

Your turn:

Your core offering (what do you make or do for others, or put another way, what do they get from your brand in terms of products or services?): _____
_____
_____

Key features of your offering (what does the product or service include?):
_____
_____
_____
_____

Functional benefits (what does your brand do for your favorite fan?): _____
_____
_____
_____

Emotional benefits (how does your brand make your favorite fan feel?): _____
_____
_____
_____

Top emotional benefit (what would be the number one emotion you want your audiences to feel when they engage your brand?): _____

HOW THEY FEEL

The reason we focus on both the top emotional benefit and even the self-expressive benefit is because emotions and personal identity (which the self-expressive benefit affects) drive most purchase decisions far more than cognitive or functional benefits, especially with creative work.

_____
_____

Self-expressive benefits (how does your favorite fan see themselves after engaging your brand?): _____
_____
_____
_____

BRAND ATTRIBUTES: YOUR SECRET SAUCE

Now let's tackle the elements that make you distinctive. Most of your features and benefits may be things that others offer as well. Where you set yourself apart is with your secret sauce, your unique way of living out your creative identity and your brand essence. We call these your brand attributes. *Use your previous homework on "your unique take" on your subject here (page 23) or your distinctives vis-a-vis your competition (page 27) as your starting points,* then refine those to come up with four to five attributes that differentiate you. Let's start with an example.

I mentioned earlier about working with a writer, a psychologist, who is writing a series of books that help people understand how culture shapes their identity. Her essence is, "Connecting agency, identity, and culture" which she shortens to "Culture." For her attributes, we framed them by answering the question, "What's your distinctive way of connecting agency, identity, and culture?" Her brand does this by:

- Integrating science with creativity
- Embracing mystery
- Evoking wonder
- Honoring diversity

See how each of those helps inform what she means by "connecting agency, identity, and culture"?

Your attributes may be similar to your personality traits, but should be more distinctive. *Think of personality traits as just that: they represent your personality. But attributes represent the character of your brand.* You may have a personality that is gregarious, charming, humorous,

DO THIS
Your brand attributes define what makes you unique. Any one of them alone may not be distinctive, but put them all together and you have a recipe for defining your distinctive approach to your creative work.

 Insight

BRAND ATTRIBUTES VS. BRAND PERSONALITY

Your brand attributes are more like your character traits. They reflect your values, morals, and principles that guide your decisions. Your personality is more about outward traits and behaviors. You can usually make a list of one-word personality traits, but character traits often require a few words to explain. Don't get hung up on the definitions. Just focus on trying to find brand attributes that reflect your distinction and your values well.

and nimble. But your character traits might be representations of your values, only explained with some distinction.

Let's say one of your values is hard work. And let's say you're starting a catering business with an essence of "Coming Home" which is a play on the idea that you come to their homes but also that you specialize in home style comfort food. The corresponding attribute related to the value of hard work might be, "Go the distance." It too is a play on words meaning that you'll bring food to any destination (for a fee, of course) and that you'll do almost anything to make the customer's event go well. If you just said, "hard working" that wouldn't convey the geographical reach or the commitment to your customer's success.

Your attributes don't have to be clever phrases like that, but the more interesting, the more memorable. But with "Coming Home," you could play off that phrase with brief statements for your attributes, such as:

- tasteful diligence,
- casual sophistication,
- quantity AND quality (if large portions are your thing), and
- welcoming presence.

Or even simpler with the basics:

- hardworking,
- willing to travel,
- artful,
- demonstrated value, and
- thoughtful.

There are many ways you can phrase these attributes. It all comes down to which will be most meaningful to you and eventually (when you translate these to external messaging) to your audience.

If you're struggling with coming up with your brand attributes, ask yourself this: ***How would your favorite fan (the one that knows your brand really well) describe it?*** Of course, they might use terms like "wonderful" or "professional" or others that aren't too distinctive. But what would be the words or very short phrases they might use to describe what makes you different?

Or try this: try to list the attributes from some famous creators. For example, for anime director Hayao Miyazaki you might think of nature-focused, sense of wonder, bright colors, or keen imagination. For author Neil Gaiman, his attributes might include dark fantasy, the power of mythology, complex emotions, or deep grasp of human nature. For singer/songwriter Dolly Parton, her attributes could be resilience, glamour, connection to her southern roots, or emphasis on storytelling.

Finally, you can use any ideas you had on "your unique take," your proof points, or even on your specialty here to help clarify your differentiating attributes. Just remember that you want these to be true about your brand, but they can also be like stretch goals in that they can be slightly aspirational. It may help to frame it this way: *What are the attributes of your brand when you're operating at your best?* That way, they will be mostly true even if you don't exemplify them all the time.

Give it a shot. List four to five attributes (the unique ways you carry out or demonstrate your essence) here:

Attribute 1: _____

Attribute 2: _____

Attribute 3: _____

Attribute 4: _____

Attribute 5: _____

BRAND PERSONALITY AND VOICE

You already have your personality traits from the DISCOVER phase (page 22), so list those here:

- _____
- _____
- _____
- _____
- _____
- _____

Tip

BRAND BEHAVIORS

Use your brand attributes to create a set of "brand behaviors," ways of acting based on your brand. These don't matter as much when it's just you, but if you add staff, having everyone behaving around a shared set of values or expectations can be critical.

Essential

DO THIS

A clear, authentic, and distinctive voice is vital because how you say something matters as much as what you say.

 **Tip**

WHAT YOU DISCOVER

Many creatives obsess about voice and style, fearful they'll never find their own. But each comes with practice. Rarely do you define your style intellectually, then pursue it. Most people discover it by emulating the styles of others they admire, taking bits and pieces from many, then elevating the parts that appeal to them. Your voice and style will come. But only through practice, not by worrying about them.

VOICE: Your message or content is *what* you say. Your voice is *how* you say it.

Now let's take the top three or four and use them as voice characteristics. But before we do, I need to clarify a tricky topic for you: Brand vs. Voice vs. Style. As a creative, and especially if you're an artist, you've likely heard all these used interchangeably. To hopefully clarify them for you, I will give you my interpretations. Just keep in mind that if someone else uses the terms differently, that's okay. But here's my understanding:

- **Brand** is the overarching concept that encompasses both voice and style. It's the total associations and perceptions that people have with and about you. Your brand, like your voice or style, is unique to you, just like your fingerprints or signature. Why I put brand at the top of the pack is because brands are about your audiences as well as you. And as we've seen, if you create with little concern about your audience, you're either an amateur or a genius. And in all my years, I haven't run across too many of the latter who can make a living by ignoring their audiences.

- **Voice** is exactly that, the way you sound, write, and speak. I hear many visual artists talk about finding their artistic voice while referring to their paintings, but that mixes metaphors, doesn't it? Voice (and style) are super hard to define. You have to try a lot of different approaches until you find the one that works for you. But it's the difference between the short, clipped sentences of Hemingway and the paragraph-long ones of Faulkner. Or between the punctuation-free writing of Cormac McCarthy and the precise details of Anthony Doerr. Or compare the writing of Toni Morrison to Ann Patchett, both in subject and language, and you understand that each has a distinctive voice.

- **Style** is the visual equivalent of voice. It's how you can always recognize a Botticelli even if you're not sure if another painting is by contemporaries such as Raphael or Titian. It's why you know a Georgia O'Keefe when you see one (assuming you are familiar with 20th century painting) or a Van Gogh. It could be based on medium, technique, color, subject matter, brush strokes, or dozens of other variants. As with voice, style also gets confused because it is often used in fashion. The two are similar since both are visual. But your sense of style in terms of wardrobe and mannerisms isn't quite the same as your artistic sense of style (the unique way you approach your medium).

The point here isn't to get into precise definitions. It's to explain why you'll need to **think about your brand from an overall perspective as something you manage that represents you but is understood by your audiences**. Most creatives don't think their way into their voice and style. They discover them through practicing and emulating the works of masters in their field. Learn the techniques and thinking of multiple creatives you admire, and eventually, you'll pick the elements you want to incorporate in your own unique way.

But something few artists want to admit or talk about is that **the market affects both voice and style.** Few full-time professional artists are going to create work in a voice or style that isn't popular today. They might do so and lead a trend. But that's like winning the lottery. Pragmatically, it is best to find a voice and style that fit you, that feel authentic, but that also resonate with your audience.

For our purposes here, **your voice is the distinctive way you communicate your personality through your verbal or written work.** Another way to see it is this: **Your message is *what* you say, but your voice is *how* you say it.** And in today's noisy world, how you say something may matter more than what you say. **A distinctive voice will stand out even if you're saying the same thing others are saying.** Similarly, if you have an incredible message but you say it in a voice that isn't appealing, no one will pay attention. Thus, voice matters greatly.

We'll cover style in the DESIGN phase, but know this: Even visual artists need a distinctive voice when they write and speak about their work. That voice will carry over into their visual work—their style—as well. You wouldn't want a dynamic, engaging voice but paintings that seem tepid or reserved. Congruence matters.

STYLE: The distinctive way you or your work *appear*.

CREATIVE VOICE VS. BRAND VOICE

There's a difference for most writers between their creative voice (the voice, for example, that a novelist writes in) and their brand voice. They should be compatible, but they don't have to be the same. Look at someone like James Patterson. He writes his thrillers in crisp, short sentences and paragraphs. But look at his Substack or read an interview with him and you'll see how his brand voice (the one he uses when talking *about* his work) differs from his creative voice (the one he uses *in* his work).

DEFINING YOUR BRAND VOICE

To get to your brand voice characteristics, take your top personality traits from page 53 and see which ones work as voice characteristics. Not all do. You also want a nice balance of what I call hard and soft. For example, if your personality traits were strong, noble, courageous, bold, and committed, that would make for a very one-dimensional personality and voice. Plus, while you can write in a bold voice, it is hard to write in a committed one. How would you speak or write (not the words themselves) in a way that comes across as committed? You can easily picture what it is like to speak in a happy, energetic, or winsome voice. But committed? Not so much.

Back to the hard/soft balance, *think of your voice as that of a compelling character. You want a believable, complex character, not a single-dimensional one.* So to add more believability and interest to your voice, instead of all similar characteristics like those above, take some of these "hard" ones and soften them up. A strong voice might be bold and noble, but also sympathetic and even humorous. Each of those make good voice characteristics (not just personality traits) and as an ensemble, they work well together. I'd like to hear from someone that is bold yet sympathetic, noble yet humorous. The more you build in these interesting combinations, the more compelling your voice, and thus your brand, will be.

Give it a shot. *What are three or four (don't go more than that since it will be too hard to manage) voice characteristics for your brand?* If you find that the personality traits are too similar or one-dimensional, choose others to make it a richer (and more interesting) voice.

My voice characteristics:

- _____
- _____
- _____
- _____

A distinctive voice will stand out even if you're saying the same thing others are saying.

IT ALL WORKS TOGETHER

Your three or four voice characteristics work like an ensemble play, where no one actor dominates. Sometimes you'll emphasize one characteristic over the others due to context, but overall, you want that hard/soft balance to make for a more interesting—and distinctive—voice.

BRAND POSITIONING STATEMENT

You're almost done with your brand identity. A final step is your brand positioning statement. It uses the following format:

For _____ (target audience),

_____ (brand name)

is the _____ (key adjective)

_____ (category),

that _____ (benefits statement)

because of its _____ (reasons to believe).

This positioning statement positions your brand in the marketplace vis-a-vis your competition. I've found it to be even more useful for creatives as a litmus test to make sure you've thought through all the main elements of your brand.

To put together your own brand positioning statement, just fill in the blanks based on what you've already learned about your brand. All you're doing is listing in one sentence:

- **Target audience**: Who you serve and what they want
- **Brand name:** The name you'll be using for your brand. For some artists, this might just be your name. For others, your company name.
- **Key adjective:** The primary attribute, personality trait, or defining adjective that will matter most to your audience.
- **Category:** This can be your general category (for searchability) or your narrowly defined category and specialty (for differentiation).
- **Benefits statement:** Your promise or summarized benefits. The thing that audiences will value most.
- **Reasons to believe:** These are your proof points that provide believability that what you offer will be valuable. These may come from your brand attributes or even your credentials/credibility points.

Some considerations in putting this together:

- *You may or may not incorporate your essence here*. If it fits, great. If not, as long as the rest aligns with your essence, that's fine.

DO THIS
You could get by without a brand positioning statement. But if you do the work on this now, your entire messaging will be much easier later.

PICK AND CHOOSE
You don't have to include every element of your brand identity in your brand positioning statement. Focus on those that are most distinctive and will most clarify—and hopefully excite—your audiences.

> **The brand positioning statement helps you summarize your brand in one sentence, but its greatest value is ensuring you've addressed all the key elements of your brand identity. And though it is internal, if you craft one that sings, you can use it as the basis of your external key messaging.**

- Don't cheat! By that I mean, ***don't rewrite this in a way that sounds better than this clunky format.*** Most clients try this because they haven't done the hard work of making sure they know all the elements of the brand. Don't say things like, "For people who want entertainment, I provide thrilling plots with believable characters." First, what excellent author doesn't? Second, is that as narrow as you can define your audience's wants? Third, you've left out your category and your attributes (you sly dog), likely because you haven't thought through your category or specialty enough. Back to the drawing board …

- ***This is internal.*** Have I said that enough? You'll take this statement and use it for your external messaging later. But for now, this doesn't have to be poetry. It just needs to incorporate your key points but in the best way possible. Thus, while it doesn't have to flow off the tongue, it will benefit you later if you can make it as compelling as possible.

- In short, ***don't wordsmith it to death, but also challenge yourself to use the best words you can,*** so it is succinct, interesting, and useful.

Let me give you an example using my brand.

For people who love to journey and make, Explore Your Worlds is the experienced guide that helps them travel creatively and create adventurously because of its inspiring content, supportive approach, and unexpected approaches to discovering more.

Here are some other examples from the corporate world:

Nike:

"For serious athletes, Nike gives confidence that provides the perfect shoe for every sport."

Okay, so they cheated in leaving out the key adjective and category. But they're Nike. They can do that. Or rather, they just did it (get it?). Plus, this statement nails its target audience (serious athletes), its benefit to them (gives them confidence), and its reasons to believe (provides the perfect shoe for every sport). This succinct positioning statement could easily be used publicly rather than just internally.

Does it cover all that Nike does? Obviously not. But it works for the primary idea on which the brand and the organization were built.

Emirates Airlines:

"To frequent business travelers seeking to fly with high comfort and convenience, Emirates is the perfect luxurious airline because it provides non-stop flights, quality service, and modern entertainment systems."

Note these points:

- Target audience: Not just travelers or even business travelers, but frequent business travelers who want high comfort and convenience.

- Key adjective: Two actually, perfect and luxurious. Perhaps "perfect" pushes credibility, but it at least seeks to set the bar high.

- Benefits and reasons to believe: They've combined these elements here or rather, left off the benefits since "non-stop flights, quality service, and modern entertainment systems" are features, not benefits.

Pepsi:

"For people who want great tasting soda, Pepsi offers a unique cola flavor that is great for all different types of occasions. Pepsi stands out by being a youthful, forward-thinking company that has been around for many years."

- Target audience: People who want great tasting soda.

- Key adjective: There isn't one in part because they combine the product brand and the organization brand in this statement.

- Benefit: Unique cola flavor that is great for all occasions.

- Reasons to believe: Longevity ("around for many years") with youthful, forward thinking.

Hopefully, these examples show you that ***even the biggest companies don't always nail down the positioning statement in its entirety.*** That usually happens for two reasons.

First, they want to keep it short to be used publicly. Thus, they edit out parts of the format that don't seem necessary (e.g., who doesn't know what category Nike is in?).

Second, they're not as thorough as you! They don't address all the elements. Which is a shame because, as you can see, sometimes confusing features for benefits, for example, means not having as strong of a positioning statement as they could. You won't make that mistake, will you?

Now it is your turn. ***Write out your positioning statement using this formula:***

For _____ (target audience),

_____ (brand name)

is the _____ (key adjective)

_____ (category),

that _____

_____ (benefits statement)

because of its _____

_____ (reasons to believe).

You can write it out without the helper words in your workbook. And remember: While you want to be thorough, shorter is better. You don't have to list every reason to believe or benefit. Just the most important ones.

BRAND IDENTITY SUMMARY

Congratulations! You've now completed all the elements of your brand identity. Before we turn to external messaging, try putting all of your answers so far into the one sheet summary in your workbook that contains the following fields:

What's the big idea or guiding principle of the brand (essence)? _____

What promise do you make to your audience (brand promise, which is really just a synthesis of functional and emotional benefits)? _____

What do you provide (primary offerings)? _____

What does the brand do for them (functional benefits)? __

> "
> **You've done it! Time to bring it all together in one place. Start with a summary then turn to your special resource—your Brand Filter—which makes remembering and using your brand identity much easier.**

How does the brand make them feel (emotional benefits)?
_____
_____

Which of these is the most important for them to feel? (top emotional benefit)?_____
_____

How does the brand make them see themselves or make them look (self-expressive benefits)?_____
_____

What are the key distinctives of the brand (attributes or proof points)?

1. _____
2. _____
3. _____
4. _____
5. _____

How does the brand sound (your voice characteristics) based on your personality?

1. _____
2. _____
3. _____
4. _____

How do I summarize all this into one statement (brand positioning statement)?_____
_____
_____

BRAND FILTER

This summary is great, but to make it even more useful, let's remove the jargon and convert it into a tool which will be your go-to resource for keeping your brand consistent. I call this the Brand Filter and ***it's probably the single most helpful branding tool you'll have because it takes the above brand identity and turns it into a set of questions.*** Then, whenever you're writing, speaking or making decisions about your brand, you simply ask these questions as if this were a checklist. So easy!

DO THIS

The Brand Filter is essential when you start because it's your cheat sheet that will make all your brand decisions easier.

To show you how this works, let me once again take my brand as an example.

EXPLORE YOUR WORLDS BRAND FILTER

- How does this encourage a person to discover and create? (essence)
- How does it help a person travel creatively or create adventurously? (promise)
- How does it represent unlikely synthesis? (attribute)
- How does it demonstrate the pursuit of MORE? (attribute)
- In what ways does it reflect relentless curiosity? (attribute)
- How does it evidence gracious intentionality? (attribute)
- How could it be more personal? (attribute, but phrased to encourage showing rather than telling)
- How does it make the reader/listener feel more capable of adventure or creativity? (primary emotional benefit)
- Is it stated in a voice that is:
  ▷ Encouraging?
  ▷ Practical?
  ▷ Humble?
  ▷ Experienced?

See how it works? ***Write out your own Brand Filter here***. Be sure to use open-ended questions such as the ones above and not closed-ended ones with potential "yes" or "no" answers since those make it too easy to avoid diving deep into your brand.

YOUR BRAND FILTER:

How does this reflect _____?
(your essence)

How does it help a person_____?
(your brand promise)

How does this demonstrate_____?
(your first attribute)

80/20 RULE

Will you be able to apply all your brand attributes to everything you say or write? Likely not. But you should try because just asking the question about how you might use each one forces you to consider new ways to apply your brand. Strive to hit about 80% of your attributes in everything you write about your brand.

How could this be more _____?
(your second attribute)

How does this represent _____?
(your third attribute)

In what ways does this evidence_____
_____? (your fourth attribute)

In what ways does this show _____
_____? (your fifth attribute, if you have five)

How does this make the audience feel _____
_____? (your highest emotional benefit)

Is it stated in a voice that is:

_____? (voice characteristic 1)

_____? (voice characteristic 2)

_____? (voice characteristic 3)

_____? (voice characteristic 4, if you have four)

Now, when you write anything about your brand, ask yourself these questions. Even when deciding on colors or imagery, ask yourself these questions. You'll be far more limited in how the questions pertain to a color or photo than to copy, but just asking makes you think about each from your brand's perspective.

When you use this to write or speak, **you may not be able to answer every question** in your Brand Filter. But **try to cover at least 80% of them** in what you're writing, or you won't be on brand. At first, this may be challenging because it will force you to think within the boundaries of your brand. And that's exactly the point. You want those constraints. That's what brands do. They keep you consistent because consistency is one of the most important factors for a successful brand. If you keep at it, it will become second nature. And it doesn't take long to get used to it.

That's it! You've now completed the internal or strategic part of your brand, the brand identity, which you've summarized in your Brand Filter. You've thought through the foundations and details of your brand now you're ready to build out the public-facing elements in the DESIGN phase.

Resource

YOUR SILVER BULLET

OK, there are no silver bullets. But the Brand Filter comes closest to a single tool that will make your branding life so much easier and more effective. Don't guess or think you can recall each question. Print out a copy of your Brand Filter and use it repeatedly whenever you are doing any brand-related work. It will be your new BFF (Branding Friend Forever).

NOTES

PART 4:
DESIGN

DESIGN *YOUR VERBAL & VISUAL IDENTITIES*

What you say & how you say it ▶ Your look & feel ▶ Your brand book & artifacts

VERBAL IDENTITY

The DESIGN phase consists of your visual and verbal identities. Let's start with the latter, what you say and how you sound. Your verbal identity includes:

- Your brand voice
- Your key messaging (AKA your elevator pitch)
- Your brand manifesto or story (and different ways to tell it)
- Your tagline (and if you really need one)

You've already done your brand voice, so pat yourself on the back and enjoy the head start on your verbal identity as we focus on your key messaging here.

KEY MESSAGING

You've likely heard the term "elevator speech or pitch." It's the quick summary of your brand. **Short and compelling are your goals here. You do NOT want to convey everything about your brand in your elevator pitch.** Otherwise, it would be way too long and boring. Your primary focus is to make your messaging discoverable.

Discoverable means that you leave people wanting more. You want them to be intrigued enough to want to ask follow-up questions or, if online, to keep looking through your website. Not because they are confused or unclear about your brand (they'll likely leave in that case), but because they are curious about you and what you can do for them.

The easiest way to create a great elevator speech or pitch is to frame it around the typical questions or FAQs (frequently asked questions) such as these:

- Who or what are you?
- What do you do?
- Why should I (your audience) care?

You'll find that these overlap. For example, in your "what are you?" response, you'll likely explain what you do as well. That's fine. ***These are the foundational messages of your brand.*** You can tweak them for different contexts

DO THIS

Here is where you turn internal concepts into external messages. You will constantly be using this messaging for your brand, so take time to get these brand FAQs right.

YOUR ELEVATOR PITCH

Your key messaging includes a set of Brand FAQs. You can use any one of these for your elevator pitch, but the most comprehensive is usually the "Who or what are you?" since it also answers "What do you do?"

The term elevator pitch implies a speech you could tell a prospect on an elevator ride. Not up the Empire State Building, but maybe a floor or two. Keep it short and the prospect will want to know more. Make it long and they won't care.

or audiences, but you want to stay true to the spirit of the brand with each.

Let's go through each with some examples.

WHO ARE YOU?

Here you'll state your category plus a brief summary of the benefits and reasons to believe from your positioning statement. Sometimes, you'll focus on the "who," particularly if you're an individual or the face of your brand. Other times, if you run a small business, you'll want to emphasize *what* you are, since category and specialty may matter more than personality. I'm going to expand the examples here to include my own, plus one for a caterer called Southern Fusion, and one for a screenwriter named Anton Carrera to give you a sense of how this works in different contexts.

Here's my brand's example:

Explore Your Worlds is an outfitter of unique insights, inspiration, and resources for artists, explorers, and other curious types who want to travel creatively and create adventurously.

For the caterer example, it might be:

Southern Fusion is the caring, committed caterer who brings a movable feast of comfort food to any place or any event you can dream up.

For the screenwriter example, it might be:

Anton Carrera is the award-winning author of over twenty successful plays and screenplays who specializes in unforgettable characters and dialogue you wish you'd said.

What's your statement for who or what you are?

_____
_____
_____
_____

WHAT DO YOU DO?

Examples:

Explore Your Worlds:

Through books, speaking, and online resources, we provide

unique insights, inspiration, and possibilities for artists, explorers and other curious types who want to travel creatively and create adventurously.

Note how the last part is the same as the "who is" statement, but I've added some clarity as to my products to start this off.

Southern Fusion, caterer:

We go anywhere you can imagine, for any event you can dream, to bring a movable feast of comfort food in a fusion of culinary excellence and thoughtful care.

Here, you can see how the same concepts from the "who is" statement get rearranged and the notion of "caring and committed" gets spelled out (in a way that also plays on the brand name) to highlight the distinctives of culinary excellence and customer service.

Anton Carrera, screenwriter:

Anton Carrera crafts the heart of successful movies and plays. His award-winning scripts are renowned for unforgettable characters and dialogue you wish you'd said.

Anton Carrera could get by with just the first sentence, depending on the context. But the second adds additional meaning and clarification.

What's your statement for what do you do? _____
_____
_____
_____
_____
_____
_____

WHY SHOULD I CARE?

Here you focus on your distinctive, but only as it matters to your audience. Many people get uncomfortable talking about themselves as "the only" one that does so and so. But you ARE the only one who does your creative work in the way you do it. No one else is you. So own it. Just know that **being different is not enough. You must also be relevant.** Thus, the fuller question really is, "Why should I (your potential customer or client) care enough to buy something from you?"

 **Tip**

WORK BACKWARDS

Sometimes, the "Why should I care?" statement opens up other ways to think about your brand. Thus, if you find something you love in this statement, modify your other brand FAQs accordingly. Let each inform the other.

Examples for answering "Why should I care?":

Explore Your Worlds:

Because Explore Your Worlds connects your inner world of interests, dreams, and desires with the outer world you long to explore. We help you discover what matters most to you, so you can create what matters most to others.

This one takes the format of answering the question directly by starting with "because." It also uses concepts not conveyed overtly in the previous two questions and responses. Feel free to use new expressions as long as they all come from the brand identity.

Southern Fusion, caterer:

We make you feel better through a fusion of gloriously comforting food, our ability to cater any event you can dream up, and the ease by which we make this happen. You'll feel the love in every conversation with us and in every bite.

One could probably tightened this up, but it hits on the key emotional benefits. It leaves out the "anywhere" because that is partially implied in the "any event." But it does what you want your "why should I care" statement to do: connect emotionally. Showing that you care about your audience's needs will help them care more about your offering. Over time, you could probably find a better opening line since "feel better" may seem too much like healthcare. "Taste goodness" or "Taste the love" could be alternatives. But this shows that your key messages can evolve over time as you discover stronger words and phrases. Your brand identity remains the same even as these conveyors of it may change.

Anton Carrera, screenwriter:

A play or movie is only as good as its story. Start with the best.

This one goes straight to the point. It doesn't explain any details about the brand but frames what the screenwriter does in clear terms that relate specifically to the biggest needs of his audience: producers and directors who want a hit movie or play. Implied in this answer is the more complete statement, "I should care because a movie or play is only as good as its story and this guy can deliver a great story or script."

For all these examples, hopefully you're seeing why I call these not just brand FAQs, but foundational or key messaging. *They serve as the basis for other copy you create about your brand.* In the last example, you could take that two-sentence phrase and use it in different ways such as:

- A tagline: "Because a movie is only as good as its story." Or, when talking to producers, "Because a movie is only as good as its script."

- Explanatory text on the screenwriter's website: "Great movies start with great stories. Great stories start here."

- Copy in a cover letter: "Want to increase the odds of your next film being a success? Start with a great script. And that means starting with me."

None of these contain *all* the elements of the screenwriter's brand. They don't have to. They home in on one specific idea and build on that. Same with your brand. *You develop all the components of the brand identity not because you'll use all of them all the time. You do so to find the ones that resonate most when you convert them into external messaging.* To paraphrase Ernest Hemingway, your brand FAQs may be only the tip of the iceberg that your audiences see. But you, as the brand's creator, better know everything about that bigger chunk of your brand that lies beneath the surface.

Enough chitchat.

What's your statement for why someone should care? ____
_____
_____
_____

KILLER COPY CONCEPTS (SAY THAT FAST)

You have a start of useful phrases within your brand identity and especially, your key messaging. But you're a creative, so let's do some creative exercises to increase your stockpile of messaging concepts and examples.

If you say, "Well, I'm creative, but I'm a visual artist (or a performer or whatever) not a writer," I will gently remind you that people still need to find out about you. Even if they love your visual work, they will want to know more about you, likely through words, before they reach for their wallets.

MIX AND MATCH

You can think of your brand FAQs not just as elevator speech examples, but as building blocks. Find a phrase from one or more of these statements and use them in copy, slogans, as headers, or even calls to action.

DO THIS

Which of these Killer Copy Concepts you select is up to you. But make sure you try at least one version to give you a richer explanation of your brand.

> **Describe your brand by comparing it to another ... but with a difference.**

Now take your creativity and apply it here in one, some, or all the following prompts that will help you with additional copy about your brand. One last point: Have fun! Too many people put too much pressure on themselves to write a masterpiece. Here's the secret of all this: ***The more you write, the better you'll get and the more enjoyable the process will be.*** Every one of these exercises builds on the others. You'll discover not only new phrases, but new ways to think about your brand. So have fun, relax, and just do a lot of bad first drafts. And out of those, a gem or two will emerge.

COPY EXERCISE 1: LIKE THIS BUT DIFFERENT.

Writer Jeff Goins helped me with my first book by encouraging me to try this exercise. It's often used in Hollywood where people pitch their movie or TV ideas by connecting their concept to a familiar one but then showing how it is different. The first time I heard this was probably three decades ago when someone explained that the pitch for the original *Alien* movie was "*Jaws* in space." The example Jeff likes to use is *The Lion King* which was ignored until someone framed it to Disney (who was hesitant to do another animal movie) as, "*Hamlet* with lions." That completely changed how the studio perceived it. Jeff's initial take on my book, *Hidden Travel* was "National Geographic meets ancient Celtic wisdom." That line didn't end up on the book jacket. But it was helpful in getting me to think about the book differently. And that's what you're looking for, a fresh way to think about your brand.

Give it a shot. Your brand is like _____

_____

but different in this way _____

_____

COPY EXERCISE 2: DESCRIBE THE FILM.

Pretend some famous filmmaker is going to make a movie about your brand. Write up the review of that film. For Explore Your Worlds it might be this:

"Explore Your Worlds is a masterpiece of subtlety. As the story unfolds, you think it is just another travel tale, a collection of

stories about places far and near. But soon you realize this is about more than travel. As one person interviewed noted, "This isn't just about travel. It's about life." And what a life.

Throughout the film, this notion of "more" appears. Not more things or even experiences. Instead, more is whatever you want more of in life: adventure, purpose, creativity, relationships, fulfillment, peace, joy, etc. Through beautiful imagery and surprising examples, you hear the stories of people who never fully grasped their calling in life, but who then come alive on a trip and return home to create stunning works of imagination and impact. The creativity angle, in fact, surprised me most. In story after story, the film shows how travel not only fuels creativity, but also the reverse, how the creative impulse changes how people travel. How travel becomes not just an escape or means of fun or relaxation, but a source of inspiration and raw materials for making works of art, new businesses, or, in one example, a new way of living.

This documentary isn't long, coming in at just under an hour. But the lessons, inspiration, and possibilities it provides will stay with you for a long time."

Write the review of the documentary about your brand:

_____
_____
_____
_____
_____
_____
_____
_____

Writing a movie review of a documentary (or even blockbuster film) of your brand frees you to talk about your brand in a fresh way.

COPY EXERCISE 3: "I AM" STATEMENT.

This idea comes from Jim Signorelli in his book *Story-Branding, Creating Power Brands Through the Power of Story* (Greenleaf Book Group Press, 2012). It's simple. Write a paragraph or two about your brand in two ways.

First, write in first person from the brand's perspective, as if your brand were a person. Something like this: "*I am*

Tip

WHO YOU ARE TO THEM

An even easier approach to the "I am" statement is to use a metaphor of your brand's relationship to your audience. Here are some common choices:

- coach or mentor
- guide
- host
- cheerleader
- outfitter
- chef
- architect
- gardener or farmer
- explorer
- concierge

Not every brand will need this metaphor, but sometimes it can be a breakthrough way of helping your audience understand how you can help them. For example, I know one creativity consultant who sees herself as an architect that envisions and builds the careers of those she serves. Another sees herself more as a doula (or midwife) who helps her clients give birth to new ideas and products. As always, find what works for you—and your audience.

(your brand's name). I live to help (your audience) achieve their dream of (whatever their main need is), etc." The key here is that this is really a Benefit Story meaning you want to tell the story about how the brand helps the audience to solve their problem or meet their needs.

Here's a quick version for Explore Your Worlds:

"I am Explore Your Worlds. Too many people leave off the final "s." I'm not here to help people explore the world, but their worlds, plural, the one in them and the one around them. I live in that place where dreams connect to reality. In fact, I help bring people to that place. There are few things more tragic to me than people living bland lives bereft of wonder, lives deemed ordinary because people never step outside their routines and comfort zones long enough to realize just how extraordinary their lives are or can be. I help people to see that. As they connect to the things that matter most to them (which are rarely things) they will discover that they are far more capable, adventurous, and creative than they imagined."

If I were doing this as more than a quick example, I'd incorporate other elements of my brand identity here. But you see that by framing it in this creative writing manner, you approach your brand and its messaging in different ways.

The second "I am" format is from your favorite fan's perspective. It too is a Benefit Story told from your audience's perspective and the benefits they desire from the brand. Here's another example from Explore Your Worlds:

"I am a creative traveler. I love to travel. I used to see it as my end goal. But through Explore Your Worlds, I realize that for me and those like me, travel isn't the end. It's a means. A means to pursuing all the inner desires and creative interests that I've had but wasn't sure what to do with, or how to connect those to travel. But now I see travel as a learning laboratory, a place where I can try out new ideas or even personas. I'm free on a trip to collect the raw materials for my next creative project and to come back not just re-energized, but re-created. I no longer worry about having breakthrough creative ideas on a trip. Often, I have none. But I always have far more new ideas and more energy in the days and weeks after my trip. I'm beginning to see how travel and

creativity feed each other and I'm excited to discover more as I explore my worlds."

Write your "I am" benefit statement(s): _____
_____
_____
_____
_____
_____
_____

COPY EXERCISE 4: YOUR BRAND MANIFESTO.

The "I am" statements were stories of the benefits of the brand. Now write up a manifesto of what you believe from your brand's perspective. **What are your values? What's your "why" and your own "reason for being" as a brand?** It doesn't have to be a personification as with the "I am" statements. Just start with, "This is what I believe" from your Believe/Exist statement and then make a list of the key things you believe either about your brand or, probably easier and more powerful, about the people you serve through your brand. My brand's manifesto might start like this:

"I believe everyone is creative. But not everyone chooses to practice that creativity. I believe everyone deep down longs for adventure. But not everyone chooses to live adventurously. I believe, however, that there is a rare breed of people who are both creative and adventurous. Who long to know what lies around the bend and yearn to see what will emerge on this blank canvas, computer screen, or stage. Who realize that creativity is like a muscle that grows with practice. And who practice not for the outcomes, but because they love the process itself …"

You get the idea. Write yourself a manifesto.
_____
_____
_____
_____
_____
_____
_____
_____

 Tip

BE BOLD!

Your manifesto is your rallying cry to the world, the statement of why you make what you do. This is no time for false humility or subtlety. State your "why" passionately here. You can always dial it back later based on the context where you will use it. But start boldly and see where it takes you.

COPY EXERCISE 5: YOUR BRAND STORY

There are several ways to do this. One is to modify some of what you've done above (assuming you tried each approach). For example, you could take your "I am" statement, say that of your favorite fan, and convert it into a story with a beginning, middle, and end. ***You'll need to incorporate these elements of a great story: character(s), plot, conflict, and moral or theme.***

Or you can try this format that I use all the time with clients. It comes from *Storytelling: Branding in Practice*, by Klaus Fog, Christian Budtz, and Baris Yakaboylu (Springer, 2005), a book I stumbled upon years ago and have valued ever since. They suggest telling your story in a familiar format, that of the traditional fairy tale. In the basic version (a rather sexist one, but it is the traditional version), you have six elements:

- **Benefactor** (e.g., The King), someone or something that provides the reward.
- **Beneficiary** (e.g., The Prince), someone who gets the reward if they accomplish their task.
- **Reward** (e.g., the hand of The Princess in marriage—I told you it was sexist), what is given to the Beneficiary.
- **Hero** (e.g., also The Prince in this case), the one who goes on the journey and carries out the task. In this story, the Hero and the Beneficiary are the same person. But that's not always the case.
- **The Aid** (e.g., The Fairy Godmother, Donkey in *Shrek*, Gandalf in T*he Lord of the Rings*), the one who comes alongside and helps the hero, often bestowing upon him or her a talisman, piece of wisdom, or magic object to aid in completing the task.
- **The Adversary** (e.g., The Dragon), the entity that seeks to block the hero's efforts.

When I do this exercise with clients, it's always fascinating to see who they assign to the various roles. Most small businesses, and even creatives, put themselves (either the individual or their brand) in the hero's role. But rarely does that make for a compelling story for your audiences.

> **"**
>
> **Use the structure of a fairy tale to tell your brand story in multiple ways changing out who is the hero, beneficiary, etc. until you find a version that is both surprising and effective.**

With many nonprofits, they may start that way, but after we work through this together, a typical set of roles might look like this, say, for a local charity that helps mentor youth in after-school programs:

- **Benefactor:** The donor who funds the charity
- **Beneficiary**: The kids who get mentored
- **Reward:** The satisfaction of helping others (for the mentor) or improved education (for the kids)
- **Hero:** The mentor
- **The Aid:** The charity itself that comes alongside both the mentor and the kids
- **The Adversary**: Illiteracy, poverty, perceptions on the street that being smart isn't cool, etc.

This could just as easily have been done where the kids were the heroes, the mentors were the benefactors, the charity was the beneficiary of these wonderful volunteers, etc.

Here's an example using Explore Your Worlds:

- **Benefactor:** The travel and creative experiences of others (since I've done research from multiple disciplines)
- **Beneficiary:** The reader
- **Reward:** An adventurous, creative life of meaning, passion, and purpose
- **Hero:** The reader
- **Aid:** Me/Explore Your Worlds
- **Adversary:** Apathy, complacency, ignorance, or a lack of openness to new experiences

Now, for your brand, give it a shot. *Try to fill these roles in for your brand:*

- **Benefactor:** _____
- **Beneficiary:** _____
- **Reward:** _____
- **Hero:** _____
- **Aid:** _____
- **Adversary:** _____

Now that you have the roles, try to tell the story of your brand using these characters. Just knowing these roles can be extremely useful in helping you think about your brand and how it relates to various stakeholders.

COPY EXERCISE 6: THE HERO'S JOURNEY

One other approach is to use a similar framework, but one in line with the hero's journey developed by Joseph Campbell. Donald Miller has taken Campbell's work and used it in a simplified format to help tell your brand story. Here's his format with examples from *Star Wars*:

- A character (Luke)
- With a problem (Evil Empire or is he really a Jedi?)
- Meets a guide (someone who understands the hero's fear) (Obi Wan, who knows what Luke's going through)
- Who offers a plan (destroy the Death Star but do so using the Force)
- That requires some action (work with Han, Leia, and others to destroy the Death Star)
- And results in either:
  ▷ Success (bye bye Death Star)
  ▷ Or failure (no more Rebellion and, worse, no sequels!)

You can find out more about how to use this format in Miller's book, *Building a StoryBrand* (HarperCollins Leadership, 2017).

I like the hero's journey format since it is easy to follow and ensures both conflict and an end to the story (too many brands just leave you hanging). But I like the fairy tale format for the more robust set of roles it provides because many clients have told incomplete or less-than-robust stories when the only roles available to them are hero and aid.

Try it using Miller's format:

- A character (your favorite fan) _____
  _____
- Meets a guide (your brand) _____
  _____

Try telling your brand story using the hero's journey motif. Avoid making you the hero of your story. Yes, it is your brand, but it is best to make your audience the hero if you can.

- Who offers a plan (your offering or benefits) _____
  _____
  _____

- That requires some action (the steps they must do to engage with your brand) _____
  _____

  And results in either:
  ▷ Success (what happens if they succeed) _____
    _____
  ▷ Or failure (what happens if they don't use your brand) _____
    _____

Some final thoughts on all these exercises. First, *they are easier with actual case situations such as writing a manifesto for your About Us page or using the I Am statement on a brochure or even an Artist Statement.* Second, *you don't have to do them all. Try one or two that interest you.* Third, *if you do try them all, you'll find that the main value is in the trying itself.* By making an effort in different formats, you'll find new expressions about your brand and better ways to communicate it. Plus, no one but you has to see your drafts. Save the versions that sing for sharing with your audiences. Just have fun with these.

WHAT ABOUT A TAGLINE?

So far, we've been focusing on stories or longer-form copy for your brand. And even short versions or key messages may be too long when you're asked, "What's your book/play/artwork/etc. about?" They don't want a story. They want a hook or tagline.

A hook is more than a brief description. It's the compelling concept behind your work. For your brand, your hook may be a captivating version of your brand essence. If you do the "Like this, but different" exercise, you'll likely have a pretty good hook there. Go back and look at some of the key messaging statements and you'll find examples of good hooks there such as the one for the screenwriter: *A play or movie is only as good as its story. Start with the best.*

 Tip

PRACTICE MAKES PERFECT

The value of trying multiple approaches to telling your brand story is that you uncover new ways of thinking about your brand, new expressions to convey it, and new keywords to use for helping others find you. Best of all, you get comfortable talking about the brand using brand language (rather than your previous approaches before you did your brand identity). Try it till you find an approach that works for you. You'll be surprised at how easy it gets after practicing, and how much your confidence in your brand builds.

 Insight

WHAT'S THEIR TAGLINE?

Quick! What's the tagline for Apple, Amazon, Google, or Starbucks? No, don't go googling it. Just guess. But don't take too long because you'll be on a fruitless pursuit. Companies such as these have taglines for their *campaigns*, but the days of "Think Different" as Apple's corporate tagline are long gone. Most multinational and multi-channel corporations do too many things to have one tagline cover them all. You may be similar if you're a multi-hyphenated creative.

Often, however, you want something even shorter, more akin to a slogan or tagline. A good tagline. One that is discoverable and makes people want to find out more. Too many taglines are blah. They use words that neither clarify ("Innovative solutions for cloud-based services"), nor inspire ("Rats and roaches are no problem for us!"). Or more in the creative realm, a tagline such as "Art that moves you" could be strong if you do vinyl wraps of artwork on cars, but it wouldn't differentiate a landscape painter. ***The best taglines make you think, and possibly even smile.*** I saw one for Post Alarm the other day on a sign in a neighborhood that used their services. The sign read, "Shields up. Since 1956." What made that a great tagline was that it made you feel like an insider (only Trekkies or sci-fi viewers likely get the "shields up" reference). But it also demonstrated credibility with their reference to over 60 years of being in business.

It's nice to have a tagline, but it's not essential. Most large corporations today don't develop taglines for the main brand because they do too many things. "Whew!" you might be thinking. One less thing I have to worry about if I don't need a tagline. It's also quite difficult to come up with a great tagline. However, you're creative, right? So knock yourself out. Try to come up with a tagline that might work for you if you're so inclined (but move on to the next section if you're not). Coming up with a tagline could be worthwhile for you because even if you don't need one, you do need a hook or shorter way to convey your brand (unless your Key Messaging was so clear and short it serves that purpose). ***If you did a good job with your Brand FAQs, you likely have your hook,*** and maybe even a tagline, already. But often, those require a bit more massaging. So to develop a tagline or slogan for your brand:

- **Explore alternative phrases or ways to talk about your essence.** Try adding a word or two to take it from an internal construct to an external slogan.

- **Decide on who the primary audience is for your tagline and write one based on their specific need.** You could come up with different ones for different audiences or contexts. And by audiences, I don't just mean people with different interests. For example, for Explore Your Worlds, that might mean one audience of travelers and another of creatives. But my primary audience includes people who are both.

Differences could also include exposure to the brand, such as prospects versus existing customers or clients. Usually, your tagline is for the former. But if that's the case, it needs to convey enough information about what you do to make sense to them. In the Post Alarm example, if the company's name was just Post, you might not understand what they did from the words, "Shields up." The good news is that rarely will people encounter your brand in isolation. There's always context: more details on your website or social media pages, gallery info, back cover details of your books, etc. Let that context provide more details and keep your tagline tight and sharp.

- **See how short you can make your key messaging statements without losing meaning.** Again, allow additional copy and context to fill in the gaps. Your tagline, like your logo, is merely a welcome mat to encourage the prospect to find out more.

- **Try to find alternative words for each part of your key message.** Take, for example, the phrase we noted above, "A play or movie is only as good as its story. Start with the best." You could replace "story" with "script" then play with different ways of using "script." That might mean embedding it in other words or making puns on it or both such as "The preSCRIPTion for a blockbuster." That's rather corny, but it shows you how, by stretching the meaning and usage of the words, you may uncover new possibilities.

- **Give it time.** Few great creative insights happen when rushed or when you don't have time to reflect on them. Your key messaging will give you what you need for now. A tagline is icing on the cake. See what emerges.

- **Learn from others.** See which taglines resonate with you. What follows are some well-known ones. For each, ask yourself, "Why does this work?" Some might

Insight

TAGLINE OR HOOK?

If you do a great job with your key messaging, you may not need a tagline. However, you do need a hook. The difference? A tagline stands alone without any additional knowledge required about the brand. A hook usually comes with context: a book jacket, an album cover, ad copy, or mostly, when stating the hook in person. When talking about your brand, if you use a tagline, it can seem cheesy or artificial. But a hook—think the "Like this, but different" approach—can spark interest and open the door to additional explanations.

not work for you. Others, like the Post Alarm example above, work for me because I not only like but respect the thinking behind them.

TAGLINE EXAMPLES:

Most of these (some classic, some contemporary), are so familiar or self-evident that I'll only comment on those that stand out for various reasons.

- Airbnb: *Belong Anywhere.* As noted earlier, this hits on one of our big four drivers—meaning, purpose, identity, and belonging—that are core to all humans. Two words carry both a sense of travel/adventure and also the emotional quality of belonging. Nicely done.
- Dollar Shave Club: *Shave time. Shave money.* Whoever says that puns are barely a form of humor doesn't realize how powerful they can be when used well.
- Subway: *Eat fresh.*
- FedEx: *When it absolutely, positively has to be there overnight.*
- Red Bull: *Red Bull gives you wings.*
- Toyota: *Let's go places.* Does this really inspire you to drive more? It's not a tagline that stands out as immediately remarkable unless the emphasis is on a sense of camaraderie and doing this together, so it is more about voice than message.
- Adidas: *Impossible is nothing.* This is so much stronger than the more familiar, "Nothing is impossible."
- Maybelline: *Maybe she's born with it. Maybe it's Maybelline.* To me, the brilliance of this tagline isn't just in clarifying the brand, but in reinforcing the name. Using "maybe" helps you associate the concept with Maybelline.
- MasterCard: *There are some things money can't buy. For everything else, there's MasterCard.* Rather long, but it makes its point.
- California Milk Processor Board (CMPB): *Got Milk?*

GO FOR THE SMILES

Taglines are most memorable when they are either grab your heart or make you laugh (or at least smile). Most of all, they should be surprising. Like a great joke, a great tagline makes you smile in part because of the "Oh, I get it" factor. Descriptive taglines rarely cause people to notice, much less remember them. Make your tagline memorable by being funny, moving—or at least unexpected.

Here are some more:

- *Tastes so good cats ask for it by name.* (Meow Mix)
- *Nothing runs like a Deere.* (John Deere)—Remember what I said about puns?
- *Think outside the bun.* (Taco Bell)
- *Eat more Chikin.* (Chick-fil-a)
- *Democracy dies in darkness.* (Washington Post)—Note the alliteration and how that adds punch to the statement.
- *What happens here, stays here.* (Las Vegas)

What, you want more? Well, here are a few additional ones that stand out to me:

- *The greatest casualty is being forgotten* (Wounded Warrior Project). You immediately get it at an emotional level.
- *Help is a four-legged word* (Canine Companions for Independence). Puns can work even in a more serious context. The reason is that they make you think.
- *Nothing stops a bullet like a job* (Homeboy Industries and Restorative Justice). I love this one because it gets your attention, makes you think, and tells you just enough about what Homeboy Industries is to make you want to learn more about their job training programs working with former gang members in Los Angeles.

One final way to help you come up with a tagline is this: cheat. Use a slogan creator or artificial intelligence (AI) tool. Two tools you can try are:

- Shopify's Slogan Creator: https://www.shopify.com/tools/slogan-maker. Just put in a word or two related to your brand and see what you get. You can narrow down your category first to get better results. I'm not sure you'll get anything stupendous from this, but you may very well get ideas you can then make into something outstanding.
- ChatGPT: https://chat.openai.com/. I'm fully aware of the various concerns of using AI tools for writing

There's a reason many leading corporations no longer use organizational taglines.

 **Tip**

AI AND BRANDING

Every day reveals a new technology, opportunity, and potential threat involving AI. For your brand, I find it works best in generating lists or alternative ways to frame things like your attributes or benefits. But go ahead and try it with taglines, hooks, or even product titles. The results can sometimes be surprisingly good. I strongly recommend, however, with any of your writing—particularly anything you used AI to help create—that you hire a good copy editor or proofer to review the final piece. I can't tell you how many times a human editor has not only found issues that AI missed, but has also clarified and made my writing so much better. Generative AI will never replace the need for human involvement on something as personal as your brand.

and image creation. And I'm sure by the time you read this, the landscape—technologically, legally, ethically, creatively—will have changed even more. I do NOT recommend letting any AI tool do all the work for you and taking what it spits out with no editing. But if you use it less as an authoring tool and more as a source of ideas, something like ChatGPT can be extremely helpful as a tool in brainstorming alternative ideas, not just for your tagline, but for other elements of your brand.

For a tagline, try a prompt like this: "Tagline for a company that _____" (fill in the blank with what you do and maybe some key distinctives from your brand positioning statement or even your brand attributes list). To give you an example, I entered, "Tagline for a website that helps people travel and create better" and I got these results:

- "Discover the world, one adventure at a time with [website name]"
- "Explore new horizons and create lasting memories with [website name]"
- "Make every trip a journey of self-discovery with [website name]"
- "Elevate your travel experience with [website name]"
- "Create your dream vacations with [website name]"

The results aren't very original, but they can spark new ideas, such as changing the third result to "Make every trip count." That could still be improved through further iterations, but ChatGPT provided a good start.

To that point, you can also use ChatGPT for your key messages, hook, book cover summary, other product descriptions, and even to outline a book concept. Again, ***use AI at your own discretion and be aware that many venues, publishers, and outlets either will not accept work done by AI or, if they do, they require you to acknowledge that you have used it.*** I'm just making you aware of the possibility so you can make that decision on your own. But to give you one more example, I put the following prompt into ChatGPT for a description of this book: "Back of book summary for a book that explains branding to artists and other creatives." Here's the result with no edits on my part (and note that it generated the book title on its own as well). It's actually rather scary how good it is with no edits:

"Brand Like an Artist" is the ultimate guide for artists and other creatives looking to establish a strong personal brand. Written by branding expert [Name], this book demystifies the process of branding and shows creatives how to effectively communicate their unique value and showcase their work to the world.

Through a combination of practical advice and inspiring case studies, "Brand Like an Artist" teaches readers how to define their brand essence, create a cohesive visual identity, and use social media and other digital platforms to connect with their audience. The book also covers important topics like pricing, networking, and marketing, helping creatives to build a successful and sustainable career in today's competitive market. Whether you're an artist, designer, writer, or musician, "Brand Like an Artist" is the essential guide for anyone looking to turn their creative passion into a professional brand.

I wouldn't use this as is, but it reveals ideas I might want to consider. See what happens when you use prompts for your messaging or tagline or especially for summaries.

FINAL THOUGHTS ON YOUR VERBAL IDENTITY

- ***Keep expanding it over time.*** You don't want to change your key messages. Those are cornerstone elements. But you do want to add to them and find new expressions for saying the same branded points. As you talk to others about your brand, you'll come up with (or hear from others) additional expressions that are still on brand (i.e., they align with your brand identity), but use alternative phrases to convey it. Keep these new phrases and relevant stories in a file and add to it when new ones emerge.
- ***Keep it balanced.*** I see this happen often: a client has four voice characteristics, but over time, they lean toward just one or two of them. You want a balanced voice, so be sure to use all your voice characteristics as an ensemble, not a set of favorites.
- ***It gets easier.*** Once you spend some time writing and

If you insist on having a tagline, learn what works—and what doesn't—from the taglines of others.

KEEP A PHRASE LIBRARY

Use a notes or writing app like Google docs that you (and eventually others if your team grows) can easily access as a repository for when you come up with or hear a new phrase that resonates. You don't want to burden your style guide with this since it may get lengthy. Jot down new expressions about your brand but also keywords that your audience uses to search for what you offer. You need both: what you say about you and what they say they want.

speaking in a branded voice, you may even get to a point where you don't have to rely on your Brand Filter because you'll have internalized both the messaging (and the underlying concepts in the brand identity that undergird the messaging) and the voice. Until that happens, ***ruthlessly and consistently use the Brand Filter whenever you're writing for the brand.*** It seems like a pain, but if you don't, then all the time you've spent building your brand identity will be for naught.

VISUAL IDENTITY

As noted repeatedly, your brand is more than your logo and colors. However, because we live in such a visually-oriented world, what follows plays an essential role.

For your visual identity, the basic version of it consists of the following:

- Colors
- Logo
- Typefaces
- Imagery guidelines and samples
- Artifacts and examples

We'll get to these, but let's first look at your style.

DEFINING YOUR STYLE

Your visual style emerges over time through the design choices you make. But one way to make defining your style easier is to think about it in terms of where you are on a continuum between alternative concepts. For each of the following pairs of words, mark where you are on the spectrum between them:

Playful..Serious

Masculine..Feminine

Classic..Contemporary

Minimal..Maximal

Limited..Expansive

DO THIS

Not all parts of the visual identity are essential, but your colors, typeface, images, sample artifacts, and possibly your logo, are. Without these, you have no way of differentiating your brand visually.

Youthful..Mature

Calm..Energetic

Casual..Professional

Simple..Complex

Abstract..Concrete

Gritty..Polished

Bright..Subdued

Cutting-edge..Conventional

Friendly..Aloof

Focused..Multi-faceted

Subtle..Bold

Brash..Respectful

Solids..Patterns

Light..Dark

Cool..Warm

Now try to summarize this with a short description of your visual style using the relevant words from above or making up your own to capture your style:

_____
_____
_____
_____
_____

Style is a lot like the old definition of art: I can't explain it, but I know it when I see it.

BRAND MOOD BOARD

Asking you to explain your visual style in words is a bit like asking you to describe a spiral staircase without using your hands. So if that was a challenge, here's an easier approach: create a brand mood board.

A mood board is a collection of images or other visual elements that feel right for your brand. They could be color swatches, pieces of cloth, illustrations, photos, magazine cut-outs, coasters, labels, wallpaper samples, thin sheets of materials like wood veneer or metal, and basically anything else you can tape or glue to a poster board or digitally assemble. The easiest approach is to use

something like Pinterest for a digital version where you create a board (and keep it private for now unless you want others to comment on it).

For our purposes here, **let's concentrate on using your mood board to nail down your brand colors.** It can help to focus not just on specific colors initially, but also on color temperature (do you like "warmer" colors in the red, yellow, or orange range) or "cooler" colors (more blues and greens)? If you want to explore color theory a bit, at least a top-level understanding of how colors relate to associations, here's a very helpful article: https://www.zekagraphic.com/full-guide-to-learn-everything-about-color-theory/

One of the best tricks to quickly develop a sense of color for your brand comes from my designer friend Jef. He recommends finding one photo you love that captures well your brand. Then take that and go to https://color.adobe.com/create/image and upload that image into Adobe Color (what used to be called Kuler) and voilà! You get a color palette based on that image. It's kind of magic. Here's an example where I uploaded an image of my book cover for *Hidden Travel* and got this color palette:

The fun part is that this is just the start. You can move those

circles on the image around to highlight different parts of the photo and thus get different color recommendations. What I love about this is that you can then use this as the start and go to the Explore tab to see other possibilities. Fair warning: If you like color, you can spend a lot of time here. Other sites such as https://colorpickerfromimage.com/ let you do the same thing. You could also upload one or more images into ChatGPT and ask it to come up with a color palette and hex codes based on those colors.

However you create the palette, you can now take it and go back to Pinterest and look for images that align with or even match. If you're not into Pinterest, you could ask ChatGPT, Claude.ai, Gemini, or others this question: "How do I find photos that match my color palette" and you'll get help on reverse image searches and how to enter your hex codes into the color filters on image sites such as Adobe Stock, Getty Images, Upsplash, Pixabay and others. Just be aware that it is a fluid experience but it can be a great way to help you land on a final set of colors that work for you.

You can use Pinterest to see other color palette examples such as this one: https://www.pinterest.com/kaylalamoreaux/color/. But once you start looking there, you'll find plenty of others to inspire or guide you. Similarly, you can also just enter these terms in the search on Pinterest: color inspiration, color schemes, color palettes, etc.

Once you have your colors and possibly some images that match those colors, start adding those to your mood board. To refine the images you find, use your Brand Filter and see which match some of the questions there, especially those that align with your voice characteristics. This isn't a test. It should be an enjoyable exercise to find images that *feel* like your brand. You're likely not going to use these on your website (though, if the image feels perfect for your brand and is legally available, then use it). *The purpose of this whole process in building your mood board is primarily to help you discern what your brand looks and feels like.* Well, and to have some fun and to start getting even more excited about your brand.

COLOR

You just did this with your mood board. Yay! You're ready to move to typography. Well, almost. Two other points.

First, *if you need to refine your color palette for your brand, now is the time to do so.* If you're working with a designer (more on that later), they can help refine your colors if you've chosen colors (like many shades of yellow) that don't show well on many screens.

Second, *realize that color consistency can be one of your greatest tools for brand distinction.* Not just in your logo and website colors, but as backgrounds for all your product shots on social media, your booth at events—even, for some creatives, the outfits you wear when meeting with your fans. Thus, choose a palette that gives you the flexibility to use in all these situations.

TYPOGRAPHY

If you're not a designer, you probably call these "fonts" but technically, fonts are the variations within a particular typeface, such as bold, italic, etc. The typeface is the style of type you use. But really, unless you're hanging with design snobs, feel free to call these fonts. Everyone will know what you mean. Some basic guidelines to consider regarding typeface:

Your typeface reflects your voice. Let your voice characteristics guide your selection of typeface and font. Some examples:

- This is the Minion Pro Regular typeface. I use this because I find it easy to read (as, I hope, do you). *This is the Minion Pro typeface in an italics font. I use this for emphasis.*
- 𝔜𝔬𝔲 𝔪𝔦𝔤𝔥𝔱 𝔫𝔬𝔱 𝔴𝔞𝔫𝔱 𝔱𝔥𝔦𝔰 𝔱𝔶𝔭𝔢𝔣𝔞𝔠𝔢 𝔦𝔣 𝔶𝔬𝔲𝔯 𝔟𝔯𝔞𝔫𝔡 𝔦𝔰 𝔣𝔬𝔯 𝔨𝔦𝔡𝔰.
- You might not want this typeface if your brand is for older adults.
- You might not want this typeface if your brand offers training courses for attorneys or other professionals.

You really want only two, or at most three, typefaces:

- ONE FOR YOUR HEADLINES
- One for your copy
- And a third that can either be:
  ▷ An informal typeface to use sparingly for casual usages such as on social media posts. Conversely, you could use a more formal script font for the same purposes. The point is to have something that adds additional personality if that fits your brand.
  ▷ **A typeface** that is more legible in your secondary media. For example, if you show most of your work online, you'd want your two primary typefaces to be a sans serif (the serif being those little feet or upturned curls, etc. on certain letters). Sans serif typefaces are easier to read online. In that case, your third typeface might be a serif, one you use for print applications because serif is easier to read in print.

Be sure your primary typefaces play well together but

SEE THEM IN CONTEXT

Some typeface sites such as Adobe Fonts show the fonts used in a designed layout, such as those shown below. Seeing this can often make a typeface come alive or give you ideas on how you might design your own brand artifacts using a particular typeface.

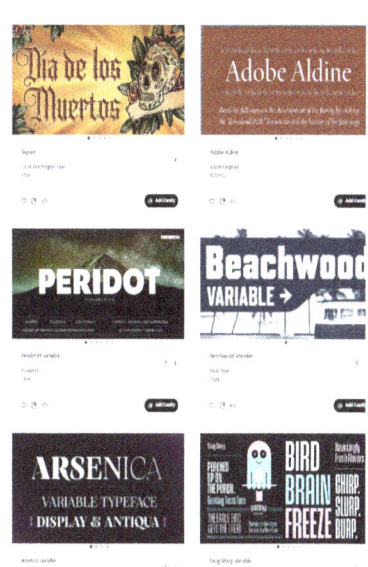

 **Insight**

Here's an example of the various fonts available within some typefaces, in this case Roboto, a free Google Font found at https://fonts.google.com/specimen/Roboto

also provide enough contrast between them to increase their versatility. It can be tempting to use more than two or three typefaces, but don't. In most cases, you'll undermine your designs and brand by creating a messy look. Besides, most typefaces, even free ones like Google Fonts, come in families with multiple fonts (e.g., extra light, light, normal, medium, bold, extra bold, various italics, and often others). So you'll have plenty of variety without introducing another typeface that might compete with your primary ones.

Make sure your typeface fits the personality of your brand, not just your personal tastes. Remember, a creative brand sits between a personal one and an organizational one. So clearly, it should reflect you to some degree. But as with all elements of the creative brand, think of it as something that represents your creative work but isn't completely you. Choose the typefaces that align with how you want people to think about your brand's personality.

Consider your primary usage. Not just as above with online versus off, but in what situations? For example, if you're independently publishing a book and want the cover typeface to match your brand's, you may want a typeface that is narrower so that it might fit on a book spine easier. Also, it is nice when your brand typeface can work for your book cover, but don't be limited to that. Often, it's better to use a typeface that fits your genre than to force, say, a clean modern typeface you use for your branded website onto the cover of a historical romance.

Optimally, if you're using a designer for your logo, let him or her guide you in deciding. They literally work with and know hundreds if not thousands of typefaces and can pair them well or offer you suggestions you'd never likely consider.

One final word: If you're going to use a typeface as the main part of your logo—meaning there are only words and no symbols in your logo—then consider having a custom typeface created for that. It will make your logo much more distinctive than taking a common typeface and embedding it in the logo.

Here are some good articles with more detailed

considerations (and links to sources of free typefaces):

https://www.creativebloq.com/typography/tips-choosing-typeface-31514399

https://designshack.net/articles/typography/how-to-pick-a-font/

https://www.smashingmagazine.com/2011/03/how-to-choose-a-typeface/

LOGO

Creating a logo—a good logo—is one of the hardest parts of developing your visual identity. Too often, logos aren't fresh (they seem derivative of others you've seen) or they don't align well with your brand identity. A common mistake is to pack too much narrative or meaning into the logo (or name even). Instead, a logo should serve as a welcome mat of sorts to the brand. *You want it to be discoverable rather than complicated*. By discoverable, if you recall, I mean you want it to intrigue people enough to want to discover more about your brand rather than trying to explain your whole brand through the logo.

There are many ways to approach developing a logo. One is to use a mind map to expand on ideas (words, phrases, metaphors, and images) developed during the brand identity process. Then, look for visuals related to those keywords. It can be a helpful start, but again, if you're not a designer, you may go with obvious or cliché interpretations of your brand keywords (e.g., a happy face to represent delight or a pencil to represent writing).

A perhaps more rewarding approach is to just *look at other logos out there and define the general feel for the type or style of logo you think best aligns with your brand*. Notice how I didn't say "like." You may like a style personally, say a grunge look, that doesn't match your brand identity. So look for types of logos that fit your brand.

What follows are some resources for doing that.

The first is to *look through designer sites for their portfolios or style collections.* This not only gives you a sense of logo designs and possibilities, but many of these are excellent sources of designers themselves that you could

Essential

DO THIS

Actually, a logo may NOT be essential for you, at least at first. You could get by with just your name in a nice typeface on your website, etc. The benefit of a logo is that it provides a visual cue for your audience, and the process of creating one can help you think about how to translate your conceptual brand into a visual expression of it. The further you get from a personal brand, the more you'll need a logo.

hire to do the logo for you. And frankly, if you can afford it, an experienced designer is a worthwhile investment since your visual identity affects so much of what you do and, unless you design logos for a living, it's really hard to become good at it yourself. However, just being aware of what's out there is a big first step. So have a look:

- https://www.deviantart.com/search?q=logo
- https://www.journeywithjess.com/free-downloads/100-free-logo-designs-free
- http://graphicdesignjunction.com/2019/05/logo-design-inspiration-55/
- https://www.fiverr.com/categories/graphics-design/creative-logo-design—You can find some super affordable designers here. Just make sure you are clear about what you want and you check references/reviews.
- https://www.behance.net/galleries/graphic-design/logo—Be sure to use the search box to narrow down your criteria to see logos in your field or that match your keywords.
- https://www.upwork.com/—The only challenge here is that you can't see the designers' work easily unless you sign up first. But you can often find some excellent designers here at affordable rates.
- https://www.designcrowd.com/

In addition, here are some good guidelines to consider: https://www.elleandcompanydesign.com/blog/2015/2/23/the-dos-and-donts-of-logo-design

Most of the above are designers, but there are also services that will make a logo for you based on existing templates. Here's one of the most helpful reviews I've found of these logo maker services including AI-based logo generators: https://www.websiteplanet.com/logo-design-services/

Now, if you're realizing you need professional help with your logo, consider these questions when looking for a designer:

- ***Do they provide a fixed bid quote*** rather than doing the work hourly? You have fewer unwelcome surprises, and you know your expenses up front when the price is set ahead of time. Sure, if you add to the scope, the price

FIND YOUR LINK

Remember, all the links listed here are on this book's website at www.BrandSomethingBeautiful.com or use this QR code:

should go up. But with hourly, you never know what the final cost might be.

- *How well do they understand your brand identity and what you're trying to do?* Obviously, you must let them read through what you've done. But if they aren't willing to do that or don't know how to apply that to your logo, move on.
- *Do their examples align with your tastes?* Can you see yourself fitting with their style? They may work in multiple styles, but is there a dominant one you can see working for you?
- *Have they worked for a client in your space?* Can you see examples? Is it only one or several?
- *Do they have a defined process that makes sense to you?*
- *Do they talk down to you in any way?* If so, move on. They may know more about design than you, but you know more about your brand. It should be an equal partnership, not a dressing down of how immature your design sensibilities are (even if they only imply this).
- *Do they have good reviews and references?* Can you talk directly to one, preferably one whose style, from the designer's showcase or portfolio, is similar to what you'd like? This has two benefits. First, you likely have similar tastes. Second, choosing a person NOT on their standard list of references means you're less likely to get a prefabricated response.
- *Are they extra excited about working with another creative person you like you*, or do you sense they shy away from design work for creatives knowing how wacky or picky we can be?
- *Do they respond quickly* to your initial inquiries? Is quick response something their references and reviews call out?
- *Do they deliver a brand book or style guide as part of the package* and can you see examples of ones they've done for others? We'll cover this concept more below.
- Optimally, *can they do more than logos* so you can use them for other design needs like your website or artifacts

Your logo is a welcome mat to your brand, not a symbol that has to explain all you do. Use it to evoke rather than describe.

 Insight

ASKING GOOD QUESTIONS

Going through all these questions can seem like an administrative pain. But trust me: Answering them will save you time, money, and frustration later. There are many skilled designers out there. Just make sure they fit the type of work you need. Finding the right designer doesn't just help you now for your logo. They can be invaluable as you grow and need additional design help.

 **Tip**

AI FOR YOUR LOGO

There are tools that use AI in the design of your logo, but while these might be a start, just as I'd hire a human editor or writer for important elements of my brand verbally, I'd let a human designer do the real work of logo design if your logo is crucial (e.g., for a consumer product line versus, say, just a personal brand). However, AI can help you get a sense for current design trends. Just use a prompt such as, "What are generally considered to be the best designed logos of this year for _____ (fill in for artists, writers, or whatever your field or just keep it general)?" It will still pull from subjective sources, but it can spark ideas for your logo and give you a sense of what is fresh now and why.

like brochures, cards, etc.? Conversely, do they primarily do web or print work and logo design isn't their strongest area? I'd go with two designers if you had to, one who specializes in brand (such as logos) and another who is a website guru rather than compromise on one that is just okay at both.

- ***Do they include numerous artifacts in the deliverables,*** or do they nickel and dime you for each new object or piece of collateral? Try to figure out ahead of time everything you might need so you can get a price on all these up front.

- ***Do they value words as much as visuals*** (even if they don't produce the words)? This may seem like an odd request if they aren't doing any writing for you, but the best designers understand that design is as much verbal as visual. Find out, for example, how they might render your elevator pitch visually.

- ***Can they translate intangible concepts into non-cliché visuals?*** This relates to the previous question but you want to see how they've taken a verbal concept in the past and created a logo around it. If, for example, your brand is about idea generation and they come back with a variety of visual concepts around light bulbs, move on. You want fresh thinking, not trite.

- ***Do they create grayscale or reversed color versions*** for using your logo on different colored backgrounds?

- ***Do they provide a good value for what you get*** (which is often hard to know ahead of time apart from reviews and references). Rarely does it pay to go too cheap, but neither does a high price guarantee the best work. Let the answers to the above questions guide you in determining the value they provide for the money. $2,000 spent on a designer who delivers an incredible logo and several artifacts (signage, t-shirt, social media templates, web landing page, brochure and PowerPoint/Slides template, email signature, etc.) is a much better deal than someone who does an OK logo for $200. But a skilled designer who charges $200 for a logo will still be better than you crafting your own if you have no design skills.

IMAGERY GUIDELINES AND SAMPLES

For our purposes, we'll focus here on guidelines for your photography and illustration. These can come from you, your designer(s), stock photo/illustration sites, or even be generated (with some modifications by you) through AI.

The good news is that no matter the source, the overall process for selecting and refining your images is the same for your brand.

It starts with *setting up a series of visual guidelines that you use to define the style of your brand's photographs and illustrations.* These could (and likely should) relate to your brand personality. If your personality is upbeat and fun-loving, you'd want images of people doing fun things, for example. Your guidelines might mean using filters (say, a retro look or a high-key bright feel) over images so that they all share your color palette. But it can also mean stylistic elements or motifs.

To illustrate, let's go back to the Southern Fusion example. If they wanted to represent their brand well, they might create guidelines that say something like:

- Only show people who are in community (no lone portraits) having a good time.
- Use warm filters to increase the "cozy" feel or have images only shot in the late afternoon or early evening.
- Maybe show a variety of settings to illustrate that the brand will go anywhere.
- Position all food shots against organic or natural-feeling backgrounds or surfaces (i.e., no shiny metal surfaces)
- But also, make sure all shots have a contemporary feel that aligns with the brand's personality: It is Southern, but not Cracker Barrel.
- Consider darker backgrounds with the food illuminated, so it stands out without garish lighting.

You see how your photography and illustrations can quickly be very personalized to your brand. Yes, this would likely involve custom photography, but you could probably find at least some initial examples on stock imagery sites that would come close. And yes, back to AI, you could use that entire list of guidelines as a prompt to see what images you get. You'll want to clean those up and tweak them to make them truly on brand, but you can at least get some good ideas to start with.

In addition, one of the most helpful uses of AI image generation isn't in coming up with new images so much as tools like generative fill in Photoshop and in other apps. This allows you to take a photo that may be in a portrait orientation, but you can fill in additional background so that it fills out the space for a landscape shaped image. This is helpful when you have certain space limitations on your website or in a presentation.

Now back to ideas, *go back to your mood board and see what images stood out there.* That's the best way to define your imagery guidelines. *Find existing photos or illustrations that resonate with you for your brand and then consider using those as the anchor examples.*

Finally, you'll want to **build a library over time of these branded images**. How many you need will depend on your medium, audience, and style. But here are some typical types of images you'll want in your library:

- ***Photos of you.*** At least a headshot that you can use on social media and in announcements, but also variations of "lifestyle" shots of you in places related to your brand (standing by your work, in your studio, meeting with fans or other creatives, etc.).

- ***Photos of your work.*** As with the ones of you, be sure to have portrait (vertical) and landscape (horizontal) versions, as well as both overview shots and closeups. And don't forget the tip of using a consistent branded color background so that people immediately recognize it's from you.

- ***Images of people engaging with your brand.*** Show them using your products or participating in experiences related to the brand—such as watching a performance, doing a workshop, etc. Think of these as the brand in action.

- ***Atmosphere shots.*** This is a loose category of images (many of which can be stock photos or illustrations) that thematically relate to your brand. For Explore Your Worlds, for example, these could be a wide range of travel shots and

Tip

CONSISTENCY

Better fewer artifacts that are on brand and consistent than a mass of materials, logos, landing pages, Pinterest pins, etc. that have no cohesion with your brand.

locations. For Southern Fusion, they might be lifestyle or general food shots. For our screenwriter example, they could range from shots of movie posters to images from plays or movies he's written to general on-set shots.

You don't need many to start. The key is to make sure that your "cornerstone" images reflect the brand well and thus can serve as models for later images.

Here are some other resources on brand imagery:

https://99designs.com/blog/tips/brand-imagery/

https://www.tailorbrands.com/blog/brand-imagery

https://designroom.com/brand-imagery-what-it-is-and-your-guide-for-success/

ARTIFACT EXAMPLES

We've noted the need for an imagery library, but *you also need a library (or at least a digital folder) for files that you can use for various artifacts.* This could be your "style guide" or "brand book" that documents your entire brand, or at least the critical elements you'll need to refer to often such as the example from my own style guide shown here. You may also want to incorporate a catalog of the following artifacts (or the ones relevant for you). While you don't need a comprehensive style guide when you're just starting, you do need someplace to keep everything you've developed for your verbal and visual identity so that you and others who write or design for your brand can refer to it. *Whether you call it a style guide or brand book, it helps to have everything in one place,* even if on a Google drive, so you can share it with others who work on your brand or just so you can keep track of everything if you're doing all this on your own.

In terms of the artifacts themselves, they are created objects you use with or for your brand that may be more than the products you make. My products, as an author, may be books, but my artifacts include many of the following things used to promote those books or convey the overall brand to others. The most common artifacts for a creative brand are these, but choose only those that will be useful to you.

- *Signage* (both external and internal for your office or

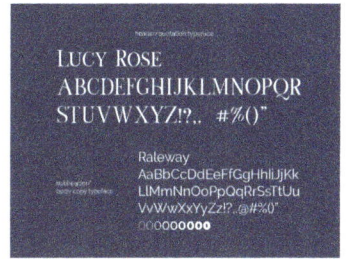

space if applicable for your situation)
- *PowerPoint/Slides/Keynote template*
- *Email signature*
- *Business card, letterhead and envelope* (though these are decreasingly being used and thus could be optional or printable as needed on your own printer)
- *Social media* (for whatever platforms you use) and Pinterest pin templates
- *Website home page or landing page template* (to serve as design lead for your site)
- *Media page layout and artist photos* (getting a professional headshot or at least one that looks professional can be a great investment)
- *E-newsletter template*
- *Article/document template* (if, say, you're offering free resources to induce email sign ups or you want a standard look to any articles you produce on your website). You could use a version of this for e-books if you offer those.
- *Portfolio design/layout* (for showing your gallery, goods, products, etc.)
- *Product shots*
- *Podcast imagery* (if you have a podcast)
- *T-shirt/wearables mock-up* (and art file if you choose to have t-shirts, hats, or other wearables made)
- *Water bottle or coffee cup mock-up* and file

That's more than enough to get most people started. In fact, once you have your logo and typefaces, you can use a site such as https://www.canva.com/ to create many other artifacts as the need arises since Canva has templates for documents, Instagram Stories and posts, Facebook posts and covers, TikTok Stories, flyers, presentations, posters, t-shirts, YouTube thumbnails, videos, business cards, letters, coasters, Pinterest pin templates, bumper stickers, tote bags, and more. It's good to glance through these templates on Canva if only to get an idea of what is out there to help inform your own decisions.

NOTES

NOTES

PART 5:
DELIGHT

DELIGHT *APPLYING THE BRAND*

Website ▶ Social Media ▶ Email ▶ Events ▶ Meetings & Presentations ▶

▶ Products & Services ▶ Signage ▶ Marketing ads & Materials ▶ Videos ▶ Content

By this point, you have all the foundational elements you'll need to implement your brand. But what does "implementing" a brand really mean? It means launching it out into the world through various channels so that people can engage with it, you, and your creative work. Not just to expose them to that work, but to delight them.

As I've noted elsewhere, it doesn't take courage to create. It takes courage to share what you've created. That means this becomes the somewhat scary part of the creative branding process. But it doesn't have to be. Here are some tips on how to make this one of the best phases of the branding process.

View your brand as the bridge. See your creative brand as the linkage between your creative work and the marketing of that work. You've done the hard part of that process. Now it is time to reap the benefits and move from a primarily internal focus to and external one.

Picture marketing as gift giving, not sales. It helps to shift your mindset from seeing marketing of your work as a necessary evil, to something more akin to giving a gift. You have an amazing offering that someone out there will love. Your job with marketing is just to help them find that and benefit from it.

See your audience as friends. Similarly, shift your mindset from seeing your audience as an amorphous group of faceless people you're hoping to trick into signing up for your email list, to a group of individuals that you'd love to get to know better. Here's a good litmus test of your mindset. If you have an email list and you send out an email, do you do so hoping no one will unsubscribe due to this email, or do you picture them as if they can't wait to hear from you? If the latter, you're on your way to living out a brand that delights your audiences because it delights you. They'll pick up on that because if you've found the right audience, they love the same things you do. And when you know that, it is much easier to delight them.

Realize that marketing starts long before any promotions. This is a big deal because creative people struggle most with creating awareness of their work. We make this seem like the most difficult part. But in some ways, if you've done the brand work and your touchpoints

Because your creative brand is the link between your work and the marketing of that work, you are now set to reap the marketing benefits of building your brand.

Tip

ADDRESS THE PAIN

How can your work be more of a painkiller than a vitamin? By knowing the pain—or deep longing—of your audience. Yes, this is easier for nonfiction books or products/services with strong functional benefits. But even a painting can change its value to an audience by how you position it. "This is my sixth work in this series" will get one response. "Not only does this match your color scheme, but it will be a great conversation starter at your next party" gets another. You're not selling out or compromising your work. You're simply *positioning* it to match the pressing need of your audience.

(see below) are strong and resonant, this is the easy part since you can use advertising or other means (like influencers, SEO, paid ads, podcast interviews, social media, etc.) to drive people to those touchpoints. It still takes time and money, but by knowing your audience and building your brand into something that delights people when they engage it, the ability to reach audiences becomes not only easier, but more enjoyable.

Be a painkiller, not a vitamin. In his book *Contagious*, Jonah Berger notes how venture capitalists (VCs) divide new ideas into two categories: vitamins and painkillers. A vitamin is something that someone needs and is good for them, but that they can easily put off. The VCs will likely pass on a company whose idea is a vitamin. If the proposed company, however, is a painkiller, that's a different story. A painkiller is something people MUST have right away. Here's a perfect personal example. I've been developing this book and course on Branding for Artists and Creatives simultaneously with a book on how to get unstuck and create more adventurously. Because there are so many books out there on creativity, yet another one makes mine more of a vitamin. But a book and course specifically for artists and creatives on branding? Let's just say that when I mention the creativity book, the response is, "Oh, that's nice." A very vitaminish reception. When I mention the branding book and course, almost without exception, the response has been, "When can I get it?" That's a painkiller reply. The more you can position your work to be a painkiller, the easier it will be to help people to realize they need it.

Find what works for you (and your audiences). Your goal in all this is to find what channels and touchpoints work best for your audiences AND for you. I love the point James Clear, author of *Atomic Habits,* made in a podcast interview. When asked about how he grew his platform, Clear replied he tried everything he could and then stuck with those channels and approaches that came easily. That's my advice to you as well. We're about to explore ways to apply your brand to a variety of common touchpoints. They will start to seem repetitious because once you've done it in one channel, it's only a minor change to do it in another. But here's the catch. You'll enjoy certain channels and approaches more than others. Note what those are. Then stick with them.

Don't try to do it all. For example, choose one social media channel to start with, not three or four. Try one platform, such as Meta for ads, before venturing into others. Focus on one goal, such as getting people to sign up for your email list rather than trying to sell them every product you've created. In fact, in most cases, I'd say that an email sign up on your website is better than a sale (unless it is a very lucrative sale) on another site where you get the money, but you may not get the buyer's email address. Having an email address from a willing lead gives you the opportunity to build the relationship over time versus making only a onetime sale.

Try marketing efforts long enough to know if they work (for you). You want to stick with most efforts long enough to know if a) they are working for your audience and you're getting any response, and b) if they're working for you. For example, let's take the common recommendation of following some famous influencer for months if not years, commenting on their blog, podcast, or social media, mentioning them in yours, and in general, trying to add value to them. The hope is they will notice and call attention to you or your work and then direct their vast following your way. My advice on this? Try it, but only with someone you genuinely like and admire. Someone whose products you buy or whose programs you enjoy. See if it works for just one or two influencers. If it does, great. You've found a strategy to use. If not, move on. Seems logical, right? But what if they just weren't the right one or two? It's possible you might have a better response from another influencer. But do you really want to spend another year doing that routine? Instead, you're likely better trying another channel and approach. Find what works for you. You'll stick with it longer and, most likely, be far more successful.

CREATE "EXPERIENCES OF DELIGHT"

All of this leads us back to this critical notion of using your creativity to surprise and create great experiences for your audiences. Too often, as artists and creatives, with a creative brand, we can limit our focus to our product. But this is where the idea of Experiences of Delight kicks in. You may think of those as how they will enjoy your product more or experience it better, both before and after they purchase it.

Expanding the overall experience they have with you can show up in many forms. This could include content marketing and supporting content such as anything from workbooks or discussion guides that go with your nonfiction book, book club guides or related short stories or character background pieces for your novel, artist statements and "making of" videos for visual artists, or shots of your work hanging in different settings so they can see how well it fits. It could be videos of scenes you've had local actors do from your play, how-to videos, excerpts, "greatest hits" clips from your podcast that relate to your work, etc.

These are ways for your audience to connect with you and your brand beyond the work they purchased. Don't limit it to being about you and the making of concepts. *Show how your work might be used in different contexts or for different audiences.* You see this on art, furniture, or poster websites where you can choose from a variety of rooms or settings in which you can see your selected artwork displayed. Or for me, it could mean creating versions of my book *Hidden Travel* for students studying abroad, for business travelers, for families, for pilgrimages, etc. I could give guides/workbooks/study guides/tip sheets for each situation to make the book more relevant for each and to expand their thinking of what the book is about.

You can't delight everyone all the time. But you can try. What you'll read in the following pages are ways to get your brand out into the world. Some of these may seem very tactical and mundane, such as an auto-response email when someone signs up on your site. But each touchpoint is an opportunity to delight. Realistically, you won't always achieve that. But making delight a goal changes how you think about your audiences and how they engage your brand. It would get monotonous (and I wouldn't be delighting you)

DO GOOD WORK

For authors, what causes a book to take off usually isn't your marketing of it. It's the "passalong value": how often people tell others and share the book. The same applies in other areas as well. All your marketing efforts will flop if your work isn't up to market standards. You can't know ahead of time what will resonate. But you can commit to excellence as the surest way to increase the odds of success. Commit to your craft. The quality of your work will affect your creative brand more than just about anything else.

if I kept repeating "delight" for every touchpoint. But you hopefully now know how important creating experiences of delight is and you can use your own creative abilities to apply that to all the following touchpoints.

DELIGHTING THROUGH EACH TOUCHPOINT

With each of these touchpoints, I'll note some ways you could apply your brand—and delight your audiences—but don't limit yourself to my suggestions or even these touchpoints. You may have many others beyond these, but what follows are the most common ones for most creatives and solopreneurs.

Email: All the marketing gurus tell you about how to set up your email conversion sequence, but they rarely describe what the experience is like for your audience. Think through each step from a perspective of delighting each recipient:

- *Sign-up form* (this is where you offer them something in exchange for filling in their email address). Think through what your offer is. How does it represent your brand? How might it delight the person signing up? Often, it is your unique voice that will add an element of delight more than the offered resource itself. For example, if you're an author and your lead magnet (the product you're using to get the prospect to sign up for your email) is a sample chapter of your next book, you could just note that alone. But if you're more playful with it or tease out some cliffhanger aspects, you not only increase the likelihood of sign ups, you reinforce your brand and add value to the prospect.

- *Confirmation email* (acknowledging they've signed up). Again, normally a mundane step, but how could you make this delightful, or at least surprising? You could kid with them as in, "OK, so you think you want this resource, but do you really? I don't think so. I dare you to hit that confirm button. No, I double dog dare you …" That may not be your voice or appropriate, but see how it takes a rather ordinary step and makes it more delightful?

- *Welcome email* (either standalone thanking them for signing up and explaining what value they'll get, or the first of a welcome series you send out, say, one per week for a month). A welcome series can be serialized (i.e. an ongoing story told in installments), a set of emails around a common theme (e.g., how to paint florals), or a loosely related series offering additional resources. One way to make it both more delightful AND more useful to you is to consider making one of the emails a quiz. You may have to link to your website or another quiz-builder site for them to complete it, but having a fun quiz where the detailed results may not show up until the next email of your welcome series can add anticipation. Note how I said "detailed results." Give them something immediately or you could frustrate rather than intrigue them.

- *Individual emails.* These are periodic emails usually initiated by your subscriber that you respond to, or perhaps ones you initiate to thank a particular subscriber or point out something. When your email list gets over a few thousand, or even a few hundred, it is hard to maintain this more intimate or at least personal form of connection. But few things are as powerful as letting your fans know you care about them individually.

- *Paid newsletters.* If you're on Substack or use Patreon to create a paywall for contributing audiences, one way you could delight general audiences is to offer a period when all content is free. Or up the value of what you're offering to paid subscribers with additional resources, access, or insights.

Website: Delight for your website visitors starts with *their ability to accomplish what they want on your site.* Only after that are you in a place to help them do what you want (such as sign up for your email list, purchase a product, tell a friend, etc.). Another way to be more delightful is to think through how your site benefits them. Too many artists' websites, for example, focus only on your portfolio or your About statement. Using testimonials of previous clients or fans can help new visitors identify with you more, as can ideas for how to display your work in fresh ways in their home, or content on how to look at a painting or understand contemporary art or other information of use to visitors. Much of that you can curate and link to rather than creating all the content yourself. But *just showing that you care about their interests and how you can identify with and help them can increase delight.* Often, that happens through a combination of your website and email or social media.

For example, on Nishant Jain's Substack, "[The Sneaky Art Post](https://sneakyart.substack.com/p/237)" (https://sneakyart.substack.com/p/237), which, as many Substacks do these days, serves as both a newsletter and a website of sorts, he shares stories, as well as offering drawing tips, and he recently opened all his content, even the paid stuff, to anyone. But what truly delighted was a post where he sketched people (see opposite) and then offered a contest where readers came up with micro stories about one of the drawings. It was engaging, entertaining, and fun, delighting readers even if they didn't send in a story themselves.

Social Media: Here are some general ways to delight your audiences through social media. This is barely a start of all the possibilities, but hopefully it will spark ideas for you to expand on.

- *Be consistent.* How often you post is up to you and your strategy. But the more regular you are, no matter your cadence, the more traction you can get.

- *Make it about others.* I know, so many people on social media obsess on showing a preferred view of themselves. But the more you strive to put your audience first, the more your brand will resonate, in part, because you'll stand out from all the other selfie images. Use some of the ideas listed in the Video section to think through ways to delight your audience on social media.

- *Be creative.* Yes, this sounds obvious. But if you're just posting images of your work to sell it and not adding anything else of value, you'll probably burn people out in most cases. One of my favorite Instagram artists is Tatsuya Tanaka who, for the last DECADE, has posted incredibly clever miniatures virtually every day.

Videos: There are so many ways for creatives to use videos these days. This list focuses on video, but most of these ideas/touchpoints apply to other channels as well (e.g., a client testimonial could be a written blurb with the person's photo, an audio file, a video, etc.). Here are some ideas:

- **A YouTube channel (or podcast shown on YouTube):** This might mean producing regular content about your subject or work or a how-to component to regularly delight audiences. But it requires a commitment to post regularly. Thus, if you love making videos, this can be a great option. If not, consider some of these other ways.

- **Day in the life video (series):** You can post these on your site or on YouTube, social media channels, Vimeo, etc. The delight comes in showing people how you work or live. Not everyone will be willing to open up their private lives to this degree, but it can be a way to connect more personally.

- **Brand video:** This is an intentional, usually higher-end video crafted to explain you and your work from a branded perspective. It can be like a video version of your manifesto or a "Why I Do This" statement.

- **Product-related videos:** These are more about your products but even so, you can have fun with them and make them delightful by thinking about placing your products in unique settings or arranging them in unusual ways.

- **Customer testimonials:** You obviously want statements from happy customers, but getting videos, even those generated by the user themselves, can be quite compelling and add an element of credibility (and hopefully delight) to your site or social media feed.

- **Making of product/BTS video:** Behind-the-scenes (BTS) videos may be one of the best value-added forms

The work of Tatsuya Tanaka (his Instagram is @tanaka_tatsuya) remains as fresh today as when he started years ago.

of content that creators can offer their fans or prospects. As with the "day in the life" videos, viewers get to know you more as a person which, in the age of AI, may be as or more important than knowing your work. Think through ways to make these delightful, not just another documentary-like video.

- **Tips and tricks:** With a BTS video, you're showing how *you* did a particular work. With a tips and tricks video (or other media version), you're showing *them* how to do it.
- **What inspires me now:** This can be you talking about any of the following that you're currently reading, watching, listening to, or otherwise engaging that surprises and delights you:
  - ▷ Books
  - ▷ Places
  - ▷ People
  - ▷ Videos, films, TV or cable programs, etc.
  - ▷ Podcasts and blogs
  - ▷ Art or other creative work made by other people
  - ▷ Ideas
  - ▷ What I'm learning now
  - ▷ What I've learned through the making of this
  - ▷ Character background videos: For writers of fiction, tell the backstory or even offer short stories based on the characters in your book(s).
  - ▷ Travel-related (sites where scenes take place): Share the places where scenes occurred in your fiction or places that have inspired you in creating your work.

Dominique Davis (her Instagram is @allthatsheis) does incredible BTS videos of the making of her reels. Sometimes, the BTS videos are even more interesting than the final piece, but the cleverness of both make you always look forward to what's next.

Other channels: As noted previously, you can use many of the ideas listed under video equally well or even better in other channels. Here's a quick list of a few other types of channels where you can test your messaging and voice, as well as seek ways to engage and delight your audiences or prospects:

- Presentations and speaking engagements (subject-specific, local clubs, business gatherings, libraries, schools, workshops, etc.)

- Podcasts
- Brochures (yes, they can still be of value)
- Author/artist statements
- Galleries (for artists)
- Conferences and events
- Relationships (i.e., who do you know who can help communicate your brand to others?)

Your work itself: I've saved the best—or perhaps the most important—for last. You may think, "Well, all this is great for my overall creative brand, but what matters most to me is marketing each individual product or service." That's true in part. But your job isn't just to sell *this* product, but to sell your hundredth or thousandth product years from now. And for that, you need a strong and consistent creative brand for *you*.

Now the best part. *All that work you've done on your overarching brand will help with each product you produce and market.* How? First, you know yourself and your audience better now, so you can align each product better with what matters to you and to them. Second, the skills you've developed at finding your essence or your messaging can be used on the product level. The same method you used for your brand FAQs can be used for coming up with the hook or summary for your new book, the theme for your next show, or the talking points for a podcast interview about your latest album. *Every product is just a fractal, in a way, of your overall creative brand.*

Finally, some elements you simply re-purpose. Your key messaging will include an About statement. That can serve as your bio for all future products, or at least the foundation for them. You can reuse your brand attributes, with minor modifications, as proof points for your products. In short, you have the foundations for almost everything you'll need for marketing your products because you've done the hard work of determining the key elements for your overall brand. So take a bow, pat yourself on the back, and get to work with your next product that exemplifies your creative brand.

Andrew Scott (his Instagram is @andrewscott_art) is another Instagram-focused artist whose making of videos and images are as powerful as the works themselves.

NEXT STEPS

All the above can be overwhelming if you try to tackle it all at once. So here's my recommendation. Follow these steps:

First, identify three to four touchpoints you have with your audience. The most common are:

- Your work
- Website
- Social media
- In-person events or connections

For each of those, think through just one way you could increase the delight of your customer or client. What would most delight them? What would be most surprising? Let's try some examples:

- For your work, follow the advice above and begin to see how to apply your overall creative brand to each product or service you offer.

- For your website, create a piece of content that you carefully craft using your Brand Filter and that reveals something about you that most people don't know or provides something of value (like a how-to video, surprising backstory, or step-by-step instructional) that is both useful and delightful. For example, I could offer on ExploreYourWorlds.com a guide to Florence, Italy that maps out places where you could assemble the components of your own custom journal, and then do a scavenger hunt map of interesting sights, sculpture, cafés, architecture, fountains, gardens, etc. where you could sketch the items/sights, photograph them, write a poem or story about them, etc. It would delight a creative person going there because it provides both a task/challenge, and also resources they can't find in the same place elsewhere.

- On social media, do something similar. For example, I could run with that idea and show photos of my scavenger hunt as I identify unique places and resources and share stories of the people I met along the way. Or for you, use your Brand Filter and come up with a series of posts or short videos around content related to your brand, almost as a mini-campaign just to get a feel for using your brand consistently.

- For in-person events, simply having consistent materials—even just a card, brochure, or one-sheet—as well as samples or images of your work is a great first step. Or go further with something to delight. As an example, you could come with small artworks or printed stories or anything related to your work and hand them out as gifts. Or do a quick workshop showing how to do the same process elsewhere. Not promotional *per se*, but simply to reflect your commitment to building a generous brand.

- Or better than waiting for an event, reach out to five of your favorite fans and ask them the questions noted in the DISCOVER section. It seems simple, then, if they are open to it, to share with them the work you've done here on your brand. Get their feedback and adjust as needed. Never underestimate the value of firsthand feedback from the people you seek to serve with your art, writing, business, or other creative effort.

Those are just a few of the many ways you could begin. Just don't wait till you have a perfect plan. Do what you can to use your brand today to delight your audiences.

Then keep it up.

FINAL THOUGHTS

Whether you're a bit overwhelmed (doing the above Next Steps should help) or overjoyed at this point, I hope you're excited by the possibilities that are now yours. You've done the intentional work of building your brand. Now you get to experience the delight of creating experiences of delight for others. Marketing and sales are mostly a matter of experimentation, and you now have all the foundations you need to do both with greater ease and enjoyment. So go for it. You have beautiful work that deserves to be seen. Your brand is how the world will find it.

TURN TO YOUR TRIBE

Quick! Take a few minutes to list five people who could give you solid feedback on your brand. Then reach out. Simple. Yet more effective than most people realize.

NOTES

APPENDIX: Brand Architecture

In branding circles, "brand architecture"—or "brand portfolio strategy" if you want even more jargon—is how you organize your various brands. You've likely heard terms such as "house of brands" (as exemplified by Proctor & Gamble where every product has a different brand name) versus a "branded house" (such as BMW where the products don't even have names, just numbers, to reinforce the master brand of BMW). Most writers, artists, and solopreneurs have only one brand, hence the exiling of this subject to the appendix. If that's you and you only need one brand, you can stop reading now and go back to making something beautiful.

If, however, you have multiple brands, or you're not sure if you need more than one brand, here are some criteria to consider if a single brand is sufficient.

ONE OR MORE BRANDS CRITERIA

1. Audience

- **One Brand**: Your different creative works appeal to largely the same audience.
  - ▷ **Example:** A writer who also paints and explores similar themes (e.g., hope, possibilities) in both art forms, often shared with the same fans.

- **Multiple Brands:** Each creative product targets a different audience, with little overlap.
  - ▷ **Example:** A children's book author who is also a Romance novelist. One brand for the author might work if the Romance books are family friendly. But if they gravitate toward erotica, the author should consider two separate brands with two different pen names even. Multiple brands make most sense when the audiences are vastly different or, as in this latter

Tip

STRETCH YOUR BRAND

The more the brand is a personal one primarily about you, the more you can "stretch" it and cover different types of products and services. Why? Because people associate all those outputs with you the person. Here's the catch: While a personal brand makes it easier to manage just one brand, you often have to do more work to become a thought leader or influencer than if you just produced your art, music, writing or other creative work. My advice? Don't worry about it now if you're just starting to build your brand. Build a single brand around you and your creative work and see where it goes. You can always add subbrands or new brands later as needed.

case, the associations of one brand (and audience) negatively affect the other.

2. Voice and Aesthetic

- **One Brand**: The tone, look, and personality behind each expression are similar.
  - ▷ **Example:** A minimalist designer who also writes articles about simplicity and living in balance.
- **Multiple Brands**: Each area has a distinct voice or style that could feel disjointed if combined.
  - ▷ **Example:** An artist who creates bright, whimsical screen printed t-shirts but also dark, nihilistic tattoos. Seeing both on the same website, for example, unless they were in two very distinct channels, could be too incongruent for many audiences.

3. Level of Personal Branding

- **One Brand:** You're building a single identity to support a full-time creative career across genres.
  - ▷ **Example:** A creative who writes graphic novels, has a line of skateboards and another of clothing, and is an in-demand DJ. While audiences like the various individual products, they care more about the person himself (or actually, his personal brand).
- **Multiple Brands:** You're launching marketable products/services in different niches that need their own identities to grow beyond you as a person.
  - ▷ **Example:** A musician launching a stationery and home goods line under a new name because it targets design boutiques (who won't know her personal brand), not music fans (who do).

4. Clarity vs. Confusion

- **One Brand:** You can clearly communicate how all your work connects.

- ▷ **Example:** Everything fits intuitively (for audiences) under a common brand essence. Even if the products are different, people inherently grasp the connection around your essence such as a creative focused on harmony who writes about it in terms of racial reconciliation, has music that emphasizes it, and has paintings that use color to demonstrate it.

- **Multiple Brands**: A single brand would confuse your audience or dilute the impact of each discipline.

  - ▷ **Example:** Using the same illustration of the person focused on harmony, if audiences don't really understand or care about harmony as a theme, they may be confused by how the reconciliation efforts relate to colorful paintings. In this case, separate brands might be needed.

5. Brand Scalability and Collaboration

- **One Brand:** You're the face of your work and everything ties back to your name.

  - ▷ **Example:** As above, you're focused on building a personal brand that is mostly about you.

- **Multiple Brands:** You may want to collaborate, expand, or sell part of your business, so separating the brands is practical.

  - ▷ **Example:** A design studio might launch a distinct brand for a furniture line that could scale, grow into licensed products, or develop spinoffs.

FOR THE MULTI-HYPHENATED CREATIVE

If you're like many creative people, to paraphrase Walt Whitman, you're complex and contain multitudes (of creative interests). You also have many hyphens between those interests. Maybe you're a songwriter-textile artist-community organizer. Or perhaps a watercolorist-ceramicist-writer-taxidermist. In the first example, one overarching brand might suffice. In the second example, you could probably get by with one brand for the first three areas, but because of the very different audiences, the taxidermy area probably needs its own brand.

To help you know for sure (or at least make a more educated guess) if you need more than one brand, here's another way to think about it.

Option 1: One Umbrella Brand with Subsections

- Brand everything under your name (or studio/company name) with clear categories or sub-identities. This is great for multidisciplinary creatives whose work shares a common voice, philosophy, or theme.
- Use design and navigation (e.g., website sections, channels, or project names) to guide people.
  - **Example:** "Ana Vasquez—Writer | Sculptor | Speaker" with each of those creative areas having its own channel (or even micro site) on your website.

Option 2: Main Brand + Project/Product Brands

- Keep your personal brand as a hub, but develop named projects, product lines, or series for specific types of work.
  - **Example:** A musician might release a different style of album under a different name but keep a personal site referencing it.
- This offers creative freedom without splitting your audience entirely. If they know you, they can find all your work under your personal brand site but each separate project or product line has its own site.

Option 3: Separate Brands for Separate Markets

- Build distinct brands, each with its own name, site, logo, and social presence.
- This is more work but provides clarity if you're building businesses around each area.
  - **Example:** This is where you might have "Thelma Jackson Studio" for watercolor paintings, books, and pottery, but "Get Stuffed" or "Eternal Pets by Thelma" for the taxidermy work. You may want to reference both on your personal site as in Option 2, or you may want to keep them completely separate.

 Insight

BRAND SPECTRUM

In the corporate world, your traditional options for organizing your brands follow this spectrum from most centralized on the top to least on the bottom:

Branded House
(e.g. BMW)

Subbrand
(e.g. Honda Accord)

Endorsed Brand
(e.g. Courtyard by Marriott)

House of Brands
(e.g. Procter & Gamble)

I only share this to show that there are many ways of organizing your brands if you have more than one. Again, ***don't get hung up on worrying too much about all the brands you could have. Focus on building the one you do have.***

 **Tip**

FINAL THOUGHT

The simplest way to consider if you need more than one brand is this:

If all your work expresses the same creative voice, style, or worldview, you're likely best served with one brand.

If people connect more with you as a personal brand than with any single product or product line, then one brand makes the most sense for you.

If you're operating in multiple commercial arenas or you have audiences with different needs or expectations, or if you want to spin off a brand or product line, multiple brands can reduce confusion and allow each brand to build traction on its own. And remember, you can still have a personal branded website that shows all your brands.

ADDITIONAL TIPS

- Start unified, then split only if necessary. Simplicity is usually better—split only when you're seeing friction or limitations or you truly do have very different audiences where the associations between the two might not work (e.g., if Thelma Jackson was also a chef, she would definitely want to keep the cooking brand separate from the taxidermy one).

- Get known for one thing before trying to be known for many. Even if this feels restrictive, it's almost always easier to build audience associations around one area that you then expand on later than to try and get people to grasp all you do when they know little about you.

- Use your personal name if your presence is the unifying thread. You are the brand.

- As you grow, recognize the power of subbrands (e.g., Prius is a subbrand of Toyota where audiences know both the company brand and the product brand but in this case, the product brand is the "driver" meaning it has greater affinity for its audiences. In some cases, people will know your products more than you. That's okay unless your goal is to build a strong personal brand around you. In that case, you'll want to do more to build name awareness for you and connect your name to that popular product.

- Tell your story well: If your interests seem disconnected, a good About page or video can help people connect the dots.

- Realize that multi-hyphenated creatives are more common now, so you're not alone. More importantly, *audiences* are aware as well. Where once having one pen name for your fiction and another for your nonfiction writing made sense (e.g., so you didn't confuse audiences on Amazon when they saw two types of books from the same author), now readers understand that novelists also write books on how to write novels. In many ways, a single brand can "stretch" more now than in the past.

REFERENCES

DISCOVER

- The "five favorite films" exercise comes from author and marketing consultant Jim Rubart.
- Many of the questions about your favorite fan come from an old article on Copyblogger at http://www.copyblogger.com/simple-blog-strategy/
- The believe/exist examples came from a source years ago I cannot track down. I believe them to be accurate, but I can't cite the exact reference, so consider them accordingly.

DESIGN:

Tagline examples:

- The first list came from the now defunct site https://pitchground.com/blog/tagline-examples/

Mood board examples:

- https://www.pinterest.com/pin/21955116928778870/
- https://www.pinterest.com/pin/38280665578205804/
- https://www.pinterest.com/pin/39195459252689607/
- https://www.pinterest.com/pin/68747803101/

Typeface examples:

- https://fonts.adobe.com/fonts/
- https://fonts.google.com/specimen/Roboto

APPENDIX

- The Brand Spectrum comes from David A. Aaker's book, *Brand Leadership,* The Free Press, 2000. When I first started in branding, this was my go-to book and many of the concepts that we cover here originate from Aaker's thinking.

NEED ADDITIONAL HELP?

For additional articles and resources on branding for artists, writers, and other creatives, go to BrandSomethingBeautiful.com.

You may also have discovered in working through your brand that you're just a tad too close to it and you need some objective outside input. I'm glad to help with everything from a one-hour coaching call just to answer any remaining questions to full on brand identity projects if you want professional help rather than doing it all yourself.

Go to BrandSomethingBeautiful.com and look for the link for Consulting to get in touch.

Or if you'd like more personal help within a group cohort, you can find out more about my group mentoring experiences at BrandSomethingBeautiful.com/courses.

Finally, if this book has been helpful and you want to assist others in finding it, please consider leaving a review on your favorite book review site. And most of all, thanks for reading.

ABOUT THE AUTHOR

Steve Brock is the author of *The Creative Wild: Get Unstuck, Create More Adventurously* and *Hidden Travel: The Secret to Extraordinary Trips*. He has also written for *National Geographic* and many others. For over 27 years, he has worked with Fortune 500 corporations such as Microsoft, Walmart, and Prudential, along with some of the nation's top nonprofit organizations in the areas of branding, marketing, innovation, and experience design. Besides his work for clients, he's spent a lifetime exploring various creative outlets such as photography, furniture design and woodworking, sculpture, music (playing and composing), magic (performing and illusion design), gardening, sketching and painting, and traveling the world in search of the best gelato.

He lives in the Seattle, Washington area with his patient wife and has two grown—and highly creative—sons. You can see more of his work and get practical creative resources at ExploreYourWorlds.com.

www.ingramcontent.com/pod-product-compliance
Lightning Source LLC
Chambersburg PA
CBHW042358070526
44585CB00029B/2981